FolkQuilts

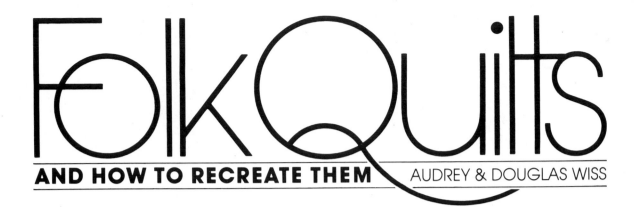

FolkQuilts

AND HOW TO RECREATE THEM

AUDREY & DOUGLAS WISS

THE MAIN STREET PRESS

PITTSTOWN, NEW JERSEY

To Our Daughters:

DEBORAH, KAREN, LINDA JO, AND LISA

First Edition 1983

Published by
The Main Street Press, Inc.
William Case House
Pittstown, New Jersey 08867

Distributed by
Kampmann & Company, Inc.
9 East 40th Street
New York, New York 10016

Designed by Frank Mahood

All color photographs by Laura McPhee
and H. G. Carter except pp. 42, 78, 94

Printed in Singapore

Library of Congress Cataloging in Publication Data

Wiss, Audrey.
    Folk quilts and how to recreate them.
    Bibliography: p. 140
    Includes index.
    1. Quilting—United States—Patterns.   I. Wiss, Douglas. II. Title.
TT835.W57 1983   746.9´7041´0973   83-61594
ISBN 0-915590-33-6
ISBN 0-915590-34-4 (pbk.)

Contents

Introduction

At a time when folk art of all varieties is extremely popular, the quilt stands out as a prime example of the traditional craftsmanship of the American past. The bold graphics and charming details of so many pieced and appliquéd quilts made during the 1800s and early 20th century commend themselves to admirers of the imaginative and well-wrought object throughout the world. Dolls, decoys, weather vanes, painted chests, and other assorted reminders of a simpler age may be equally valuable antique items, but they do not enjoy the almost universal appeal of the quilt. Quilts have been made since the 17th century in North America by individuals and sewing groups. By the mid-1800s, quiltmaking was a craft practiced in almost every home as well as in the Grange Hall and church manse. Anyone wishing to pursue this practical and decorative activity—men, women, and children—could draw upon an ever-growing repertory of designs to follow. Interest in quilting declined in urban areas around the turn of the century, but by the 1930s the craft had been revived in both cities and villages. What better way to supply a Depression-era family with warm, attractive bed coverings? And, by this time, the quilter could choose from well over a thousand well-established patterns for inspiration.

Quilting has truly been a folk art, an art of the people. The names of many traditional patterns reflect America's rural roots—Barn Raising, Flying Geese, Bear's Paw, Grandmother's Flower Garden. It has been an art practiced by all of North America's many immigrant communities. Some would say that the Amish and Mennonites have excelled with their vividly colored, non-representational designs which are so expressive of simple country pursuits and pleasures. But many of the most imaginative patterns have their roots in other traditions, and these designs have come to be shared by all communities.

Folk Quilts presents a wide selection of traditional designs for the modern quilter which have been tested over time. They are presented in their original colors and special configurations. Some date back as far as the 18th century; others became popular as late as the 1930s. A few are worked in wool or silk; most are pieced of plain or printed cottons. All were made in America and display a variety of piecing, appliqué, and quilting techniques.

Today quilting has become so popular a pastime that there has been some loss in the craft's aesthetic qualities. There is a great deal that is unfortunate about much modern quilting, however well-intentioned. Synthetic materials are often substituted for natural fibers, and a polyester quilt has about as much aesthetic appeal as a baggy pants suit.

Cheap colors—mainly sickly pastels or screaming day-glo tints—are used instead of rich, complementary shades. Just a quick perusal of the pages of this book will lead to the conclusion that our grandmothers and their mothers had a keen understanding of how colors and shapes and materials could be blended together to create wonderfully dramatic and pleasing effects.

We have been collecting quilts for many years, and our wonder over the accomplishments of our ancestors grows with time. Once we have seen what must be the most perfect Sunshine and Shadow or Streaks of Lightning quilt, there is always another to discover, even more striking than the first. It is our love and enjoyment of these discoveries that we wish to share with today's quilter. These are patterns which should be kept alive and not only displayed in museum collections or on the walls of corporate board rooms. They are designs worthy of re-creation. They needn't be copied exactly. No two antique quilts are ever the same in each detail. Their charm, in fact, lies in their individuality, even in their imperfections. Certain considerations of design govern the working of each design, however, and these are suggested in both the introductions and the instructions provided for each quilt. Where possible, we have suggested other alternatives or variations on the basic design which the quilter might undertake.

Thirty basic design types are illustrated in black and white and color photographs and are further explained in piecing diagrams and pattern pieces. In addition, we have provided information on the piecing of Log Cabin-type quilts, including such well-known patterns as Barn Raising and Streaks of Lightning. To further assist the quilter, information on where antique examples may be seen, a list of prominent dealers in old quilts, and a directory of suppliers of quality materials have been provided. For those who wish to learn more about the history of quilting, the bibliography will supply useful material. Instructions on the stitching of decorative designs, the "quilting" aspect of quilting, have not been included. Some of the most common pieced designs left little room for such elaboration or, like the Log Cabin variations, did not allow for it at all. For those wishing to work such common motifs as the shell, diamond, feather, and rope stitches, there are numerous helpful instruction books.

The making of quilts grew out of necessity. Today, the craft can be pursued more easily and enjoyably. Each quilt pattern that is attempted provides a new learning experience. Within a traditional framework, the opportunities to interpret something of your own making are virtually unlimited.

In assembling *Folk Quilts* we are indebted to our editor, Laura McPhee, for her thoughtful assistance, and to Frank Mahood and Donald Rolfe for their useful and attractive diagrams. We also wish to acknowledge the generous contributions of the Morris Museum of Arts and Sciences and of the following persons: Robert and Maryann Welsh of the 1800 House, Jack and Sonja Perry, Phyllis Haders, Joel and Kate Kopp of America Hurrah, Mr. and Mrs. Kenneth Miller, Linda McKenna and Nacky Smith-Morgan, James Gregory and John Puckett of The Pink House, Mr. and Mrs. Alan E. Burland, Mr. and Mrs. William D. Blaine, Karen Wiss, Ann Hackl and Deborah Clark of the Woolverton Inn, and Nan Mutnick, decorative arts curator of the Morris Museum of Arts and Sciences.

1. Streaks of Lightning/ Log Cabin

WHEN the Log Cabin design first appeared in the middle of the last century, the response from quilters in both North America and England was one of enormous enthusiasm. Made from numerous strips of fabric sewn into blocks, this new pattern was extraordinarily versatile; there seemed no end to the types and colors of fabrics which could be put to use, and the remnants of everything from wedding dresses to silk petticoats to shirts and overalls were employed in the quilters' creations. Furthermore, the distribution of color within the individual blocks and the blocks' arrangement on the field of the quilt allowed the quilter to create a wide variety of patterns and visual effects which came to have names like Barn Raising, Courthouse Steps, Clocks, Pineapple, Straight Furrows, Streaks of Lightning, and Windmill Blades, among many others.

The quilt illustrated opposite is known variously as Streaks of Lightning, Herringbone, and Zigzag. The pattern is made of ninety-nine blocks of equal size, each constructed of sixteen logs of the same width but varying lengths, which are placed around a central square. Two different block types are needed to make this pattern: the blocks differ only in the placement of the light and dark logs (see the diagrams on the next two pages). After all of the blocks have been completed, the quilter arranges them in rows to form the zigzag pattern.

Log Cabin quilts, no matter which pattern, are constructed differently than most quilts, as none of the stitching ever shows. It is extremely rare to find Log Cabin pieces which have any quilting whatsoever. Generally tufting is used to hold the quilt, the back, and the filling together. (For further details on how to piece a Log Cabin quilt, see Appendix A.)

Though scraps of numerous colors, textures, and fabrics may be used within the same quilt, color choice and placement must be carefully thought out in order to produce the best effect. The person who made the quilt illustrated here used cottons of blue, brown, red, and green hues; there are calicoes, solids, and prints. The only constants are the bright yellow squares which appear in the center of each of the blocks and the general way in which the logs are arranged. When the design first appeared, Log Cabin quilts were made in heavy, long-lasting materials such as wool. In later years, the pattern began to appear in all manner of fabrics such as cotton, satin, and silk. Although the popularity of the Log Cabin pattern began to diminish in the late-Victorian era, this fine versatile design is still produced by quilters today.

Streaks of Lightning/Log Cabin

Size: Approximately 80″ x 66″

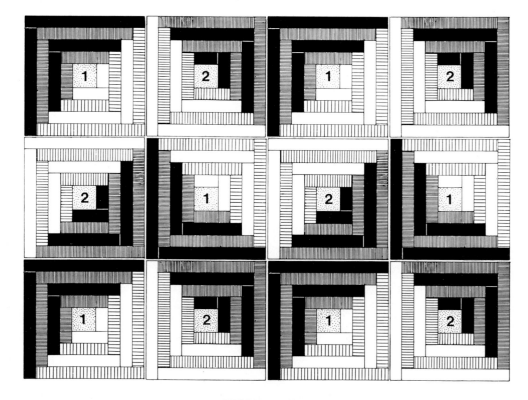

PIECING DIAGRAM.

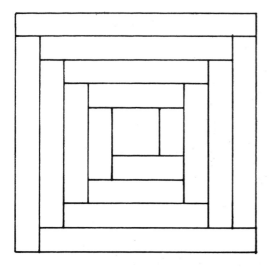

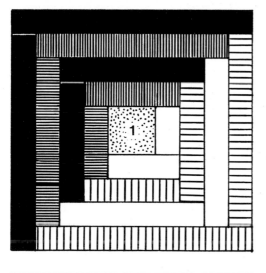

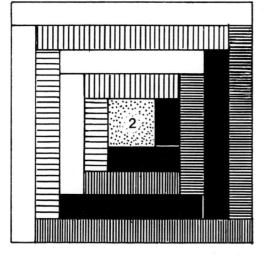

This vibrant, electric pattern is relatively easy to piece and is very pleasing when completed. Two types of Log Cabin blocks are required for this design: In block 1 the two outer logs are dark; in block 2 they are light. All in all, ninety-nine blocks are required; they are arranged in rows nine across and eleven down. Once they are pieced in the order indicated in the piecing diagram (left), they combine to form the zigzags known as Streaks of Lightning.

Each block is 7¼″ square. The center piece is 1½″ square. The individual logs are ¾″ wide and of varying lengths. The logs should be 1¼″ wide when they are cut so that there is plenty of room allowed for making the seams. Altogether, sixteen logs are used in each block. (A full-size piecing diagram for a Streaks of Lightning block appears in Appendix A).

This quilter used neither a border nor a binding to frame her quilt. The edges of the quilt are simply the logs of the blocks. Log Cabin quilts almost never have wide or quilted borders, though they usually do have a plain binding and/or border to protect the edges from wear.

2. Crossbars

Although the Crossbars quilt illustrated opposite was made as late as 1920, the simplicity of its construction and design gives it an older appearance. An uncomplicated pattern, it has been known since the first colonists arrived in the New World. Very few antique examples have survived, however, for Crossbars quilts were used for everyday bed coverings, and most fabrics cannot withstand heavy use over a long period of time. This particular quilt was made by an Indiana Amish quilter or quilters and exemplifies the Amish talent for mixing somber colors with bright, saturated ones to produce a vivid and compelling composition. The unusual color choices—lavender, black, white, salmon, pale green, and blue—are enormously effective: the electric shade of salmon makes the whole quilt dance.

Crossbars is constructed of bars made up of many strips of fabric which surround large squares of the background color (in this case, a rich blue-gray). The bars consist of small multi-colored rectangular pieces of varying widths but the same length, placed adjacent to each other in random order. A small square of contrasting color (white in the quilt illustrated) is pieced at the intersections of the bars. These white squares and the large central squares around which the composition is built allow ample room for the practice of any quilting method—from simple block quilting to more intricate designs such as wreaths, flowers, or rope.

There are few variations of Crossbars, though slight design changes can radically alter the appearance of the quilt. A window-pane effect may be achieved by narrowing the width of the strips in the bars. More colors can be introduced, or the quilt might be composed of just two or three alternating colors. The bars may be cut to a standard width, and designs can be appliquéd within the large squares. Great freedom of color choice and uncomplicated design make this pattern an excellent one for the beginning quilter to recreate.

Crossbars

<small>SIZE:</small> Approximately 61″ x 75″

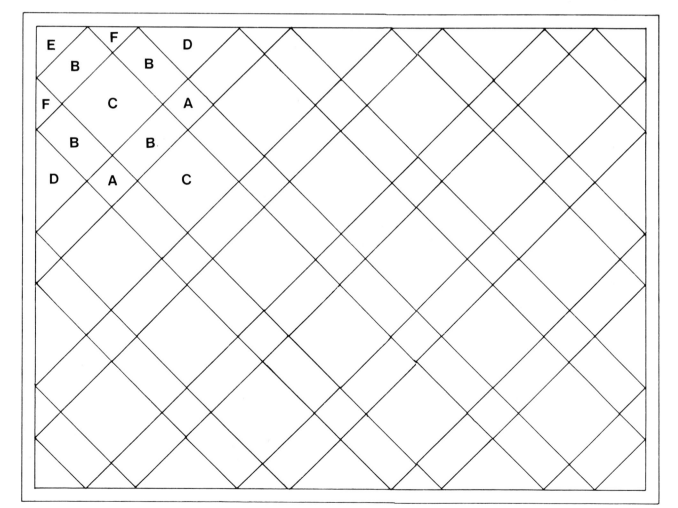

PIECING DIAGRAM.

A simple yet classic design, Crossbars provides an attractive and unusual pattern for the novice quilter to re-create. Extremely easy to piece, the design is made from plain squares of two sizes (A is 4″ x 4″, C is 8″ x 8″) and 8″ x 4″ bars (B) which are pieced from strips of several colors and varying widths. (See full-size piecing diagram, left.) Seventeen "A" pieces, forty-eight "B", and eighteen "C" pieces are needed.

Piece "D" is made by cutting a "C" square on the diagonal; "F" is cut in the same manner from "A". "E" is made by folding "D" in half and cutting it in two. For all these pieces, be sure to leave an extra ¼″ for the seams. Ten "D", four "E", and fourteen "F" pieces are required to finish the design area.

An inner border ⅜″ wide frames the composition. The outer border is 5″ wide on the sides and 3″ on the top and bottom. Without the bright inner border, this composition would not be half as appealing.

This quilter chose to use cotton fabrics of solid colors throughout the design, but more contemporary pieces could be done in printed or patterned fabric of almost any type. Before undertaking this project, however, the maker may want to piece an 8″ x 4″ bar to see if the chosen colors are truly harmonious.

B PIECING DIAGRAM.

3. Variable Star

ONE of the most appealing and popular quilt motifs, the star appears in many forms, and at least 100 patterns carry this celestial name. The version shown here is known as Variable Star, Evening Star, or Simple Star. As the last name indicates, the form is straightforward in design and exceptionally easy to piece. Variable Star, one of the oldest quilt patterns, has been produced by North American quilters for well over two centuries. The majority of antique examples are of cotton, as they were most often made for daily use, though pieces done in rare and expensive fabrics can be found.

The quilt pictured here, made in the gently rolling farm country of Eastern Pennsylvania toward the close of the last century, is constructed of yellow, black, blue, red, and tan cotton calicoes and a bright crimson solid. To piece an individual star patch, the quilter begins with a square, to which four smaller squares, eight half-squares, and four triangles are attached (see the following two pages for details). In this example the central square and the half-squares which form the star points are of the same fabric; in other versions of this pattern the squares and points are of contrasting colors. The graphic patches are set on the diagonal, and arranged in rows six across and five down. Plain squares of the background fabric alternate with the graphic patches. The composition is framed with a pieced border constructed of half-squares; here crimson alternates with tan: The visual effect is heightened delightfully by the addition of a sawtooth border.

Variable Stars can be embellished in many ways. Feathered Star (see Chapter 14) is a more complicated version of this form. Very delicate in appearance, it is also far more difficult to piece. The simpler Variable Star is recommended for the beginning quilter.

Variable Star

Sɪᴢᴇ: Approximately 81″ x 91″

Variable or Simple Star is one of the easiest of folk quilt patterns to recreate. This one, with its wonderful sawtooth border, is large enough for a double bed.

PIECING DIAGRAM.

Thirty 7″ x 7″ graphic patches and the same number of plain patches are required. We suggest that the quilter begin by tracing the four basic pattern pieces (A, B, C, D) from the full-size piecing diagram. The tracings should be transferred onto cardboard and then cut out to make templates. The ¼″ necessary for the seam allowance can be added to the template or added when cutting the fabric.

SECTIONAL PIECING DIAGRAM.

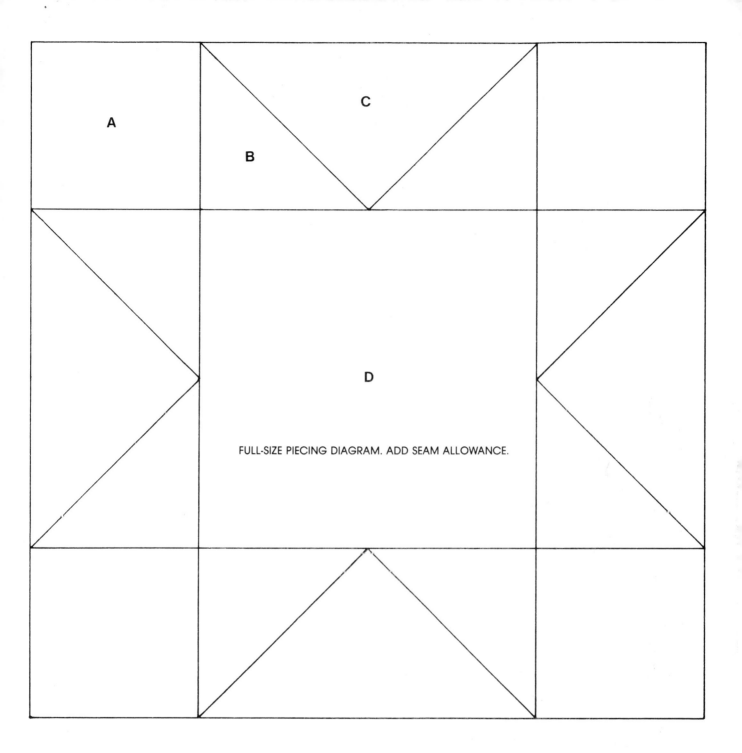

A

B

C

D

FULL-SIZE PIECING DIAGRAM. ADD SEAM ALLOWANCE.

To begin, two "B" pieces are sewn to each of the four "C" pieces. Then the resulting rectangular pieces are added to the central "D" square. Four "A" pieces sewn into each corner finish the block. Once the thirty blocks are completed, they are set on the diagonal and sewed to the plain patches.

The sawtooth border which surrounds the central area of the composition is made entirely of "C" pieces in two colors. The wide outer border (which, in this case, is the same color as the plain patches) measures approximately 12".

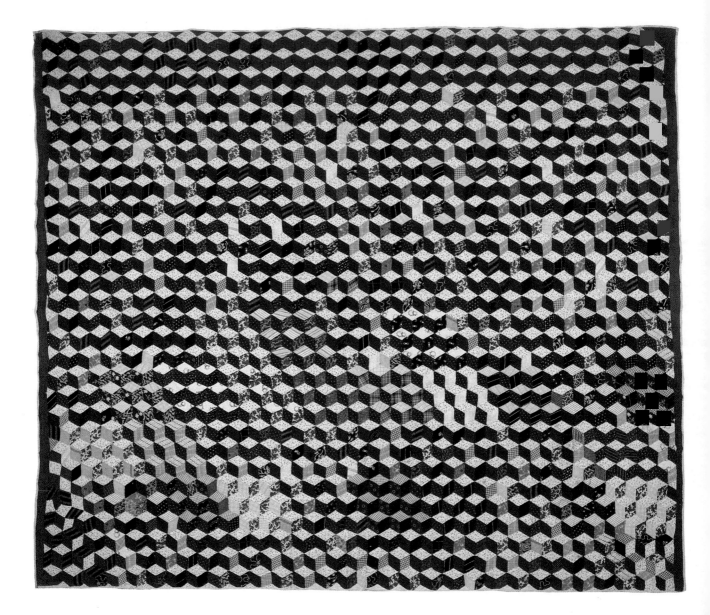

4. Tumbling Blocks

A VARIATION of the two-dimensional one-patch, Tumbling Blocks is a pattern which seems to add a third dimension to quilting. By careful color choice and placement, the illusion of rows of three-dimensional blocks can be created. Piecing of this quilt is not extraordinarily difficult, but must be thought out carefully in advance, and the hundreds of little diamonds must be cut and sewn as methodically as possible or the quilt will not lie flat.

While the tumbling blocks appear to be square, each one is actually formed from three diamond-shaped pieces. Generally this effect is achieved by piecing a medium-colored and a dark-colored diamond side to side, and then filling in the top with a light-colored piece. The blocks then appear three-dimensional, whether the quilt is viewed from the top, bottom, or side.

The quilter who constructed the example illustrated here did not always stick to the pattern. In several places there are extra light diamonds which destroy the illusion of the third dimension. Perhaps the maker did this in order to relieve the monotony a bit; perhaps it was done in response to the once-common belief that human beings might offend God by making an earthly work too perfect. More likely, however, the quilter was inexperienced and simply lost track of the pattern. Touches such as these—accidental or not—are what give life and charm to so many examples of American folk art.

A favorite pattern among quilters throughout North America since the late 18th century, Tumbling Blocks has been pieced in all common fabrics and in all appropriate bed sizes. Both Calvin Coolidge and Dwight D. Eisenhower are known to have helped make quilts of this design as children. The examples of their handiwork can be seen today, and testify to their considerable skill.

An exciting variation of Tumbling Blocks is called Stairway to Heaven or Stair of Illusion. In this pattern the contrasting rows of colored blocks are placed on the diagonal to form a pyramid. If Tumbling Blocks is constructed with large diamond shapes, rather than the traditional small ones, it is sometimes referred to as Baby Blocks or Building Blocks.

Tumbling Blocks

Sɪᴢᴇ: Approximately 67″ x 76″

Tumbling Blocks is relatively easy to piece and should be made row by horizontal row. The antique example illustrated in the color plate was made with tinier pieces then the full-size pattern pieces provided here, and the original quilter made many more blocks per row than are presently sug-

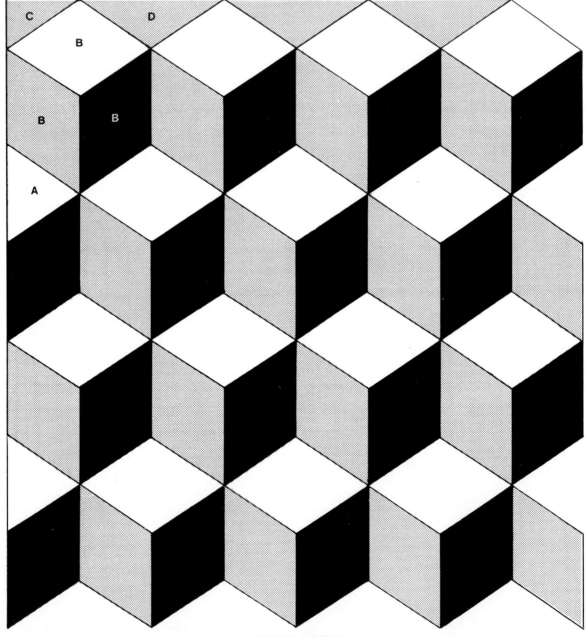

PIECING DIAGRAM.

gested. The modern maker may wish to use the full-size pattern pieces provided, as the large size makes them somewhat easier to cut and sew. The quilt suggested, when finished, should be fifteen tumbling blocks wide and fifteen blocks long.

To begin, the quilter joins a row of alternating medium and dark diamond-shaped pieces (B). The seams are left open at the top and bottom, and when the row is completed, the quilter adds light "B" pieces in the V-shaped areas left by the joined diamond shapes. If the quilter who made the piece illustrated here had worked with complete regularity, red would alternate with dark blue and a white and tan calico would fill all the V-shaped areas.

The arrangement of full-size pattern pieces (below) illustrates the method of piecing the lower righthand corner of the quilt. The "C" piece fills the corner, and half-diamonds (D) are placed all along both the lower and upper edge of the quilt. (At the top, they are inverted, of course). "A" pieces are pieced on both edges of the quilt.

The red border on two sides is 2″ wide. The binding is about $\frac{3}{16}$″.

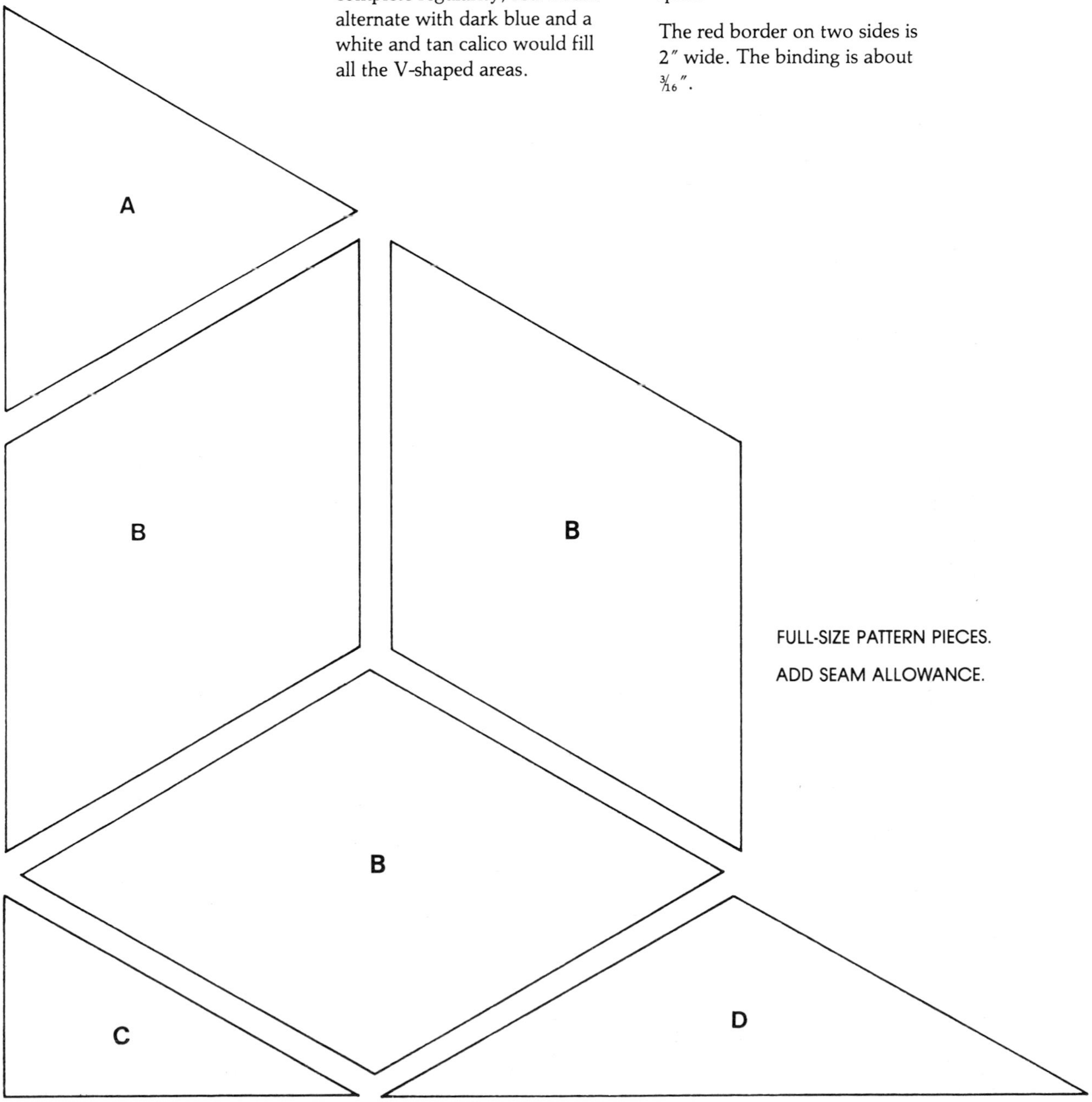

A

B

B

B

FULL-SIZE PATTERN PIECES.

ADD SEAM ALLOWANCE.

C

D

5. Windmill Blades

MADE in Monmouth County, New Jersey, around 1870, the quilt illustrated opposite reflects the Victorian love of rich fabrics and dramatic colors. This example of the Windmill Blades pattern is pieced of silk and is in exceptionally fine condition. Silk does not withstand use and age as well as cotton, and today it is considered a coup to discover an antique silk quilt not in need of an extremely costly restoration.

The quilter who made this piece chose black as the background color—an unusual but effective design decision. The brilliantly colored windmill blades stand out in striking contrast to the somber background. This quilt was probably intended for special occasions rather than for everyday use—it is quite small—but Windmill Blades has been executed in a wide variety of sizes, colors, and fabrics by the Amish and Mennonites, as well as by other quilters throughout North America.

The dimensions of the individual blocks in the Windmill Blades pattern can vary radically from piece to piece. In this example, there are numerous logs used in each of the four blades and four background sections, and the blocks are quite large. The many logs used in this piece are evidence of the maker's expertise; a less ambitious quilter might use as few as five logs per section. Essentially an eight-sided Log Cabin block, Windmill Blades must be cut and sewn precisely to produce the optimum effect. (For further information on piecing Log Cabin quilts, see Appendix A.)

Windmill Blades is one of the most challenging and complicated Log Cabin patterns to construct, and is prized by collectors both for its bold and vital design and because antique examples are so difficult to find. A charming variation on the Windmill Blades theme is a pattern known as Pineapple. Each block of a Pineapple quilt—differing from Windmill Blades in the choice and placement of color—is generally smaller and constructed of fewer logs so that it more closely resembles the shape of the fruit. Other variations can be made by altering the color arrangement of the bars. Alternating or non-repeating colors are sometimes used to achieve a graphic effect entirely different from that of the quilt illustrated here.

Windmill Blades

Size: Approximately 50″ x 65″

One of the most complicated of Log Cabin designs, the Windmill Blades pattern employs eight-sided rather than the usual four-sided blocks. The blade effect is achieved by piecing the four short sides in a dark background color (in this case, black). These stand in stark contrast to the four brightly colored "blades."

This quilter made twelve 15″ eight-sided blocks and pieced them side by side. To piece the individual blocks, the maker begins with a 1½″ square (A) which forms the epicenter of the whirling blades. Piece "B" is the pattern for the four isosceles triangles (1½″ base and 1⅛″ sides) which are sewn next to the square. Then the strips or logs are cut out and sewn together. Each of the four blades in each block requires eleven strips; nine are needed for the background area. The strips are all ¾″ wide (1¼″ with seam allowance) and of varying lengths. Isosceles triangles (C) with 2½″ bases and 1¾″ sides fill in the four corner of the square. The border which frames the quilt is approximately 2½″ wide.

Blocks made with fewer strips can be just as effective as more complicated ones. The novice quilter should try a practice block first. After piecing five strips on each of the eight sides, stop to see if the design has the desired appearance. The modern quilter may prefer many small blocks to just a few large ones.

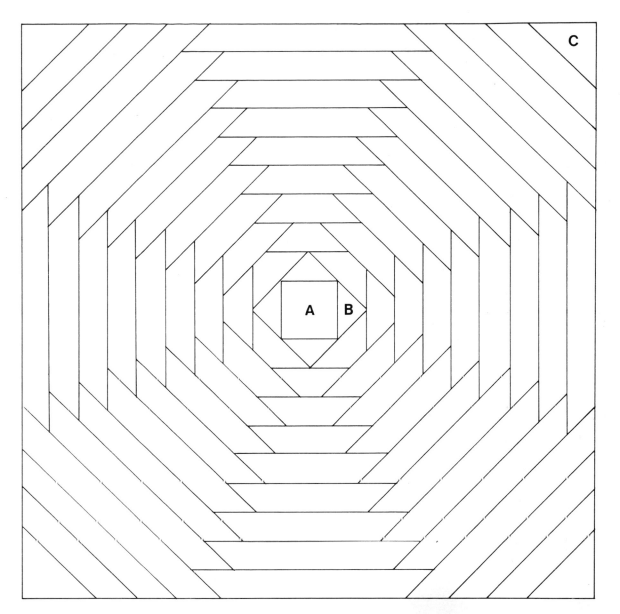

PIECING DIAGRAM.

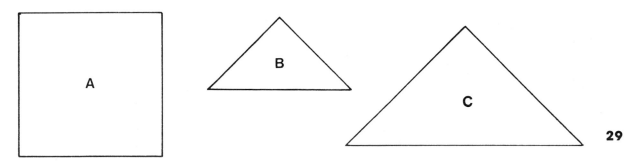

FULL-SIZE PATTERN PIECES. ADD SEAM ALLOWANCE.

29

6. Dresden Plate

First made in the 19th century, the Dresden Plate pattern reached the height of its popularity in the 1920s and '30s, when large numbers of quilt kits were produced for inexperienced seamstresses all over North America. The theme and its variations seem to have had great appeal, for quilts of this pattern, executed in the stylish pastel solids and prints popular in the early 1900s, abound today.

The quilt illustrated on the opposite page was made by a New Jersey quilter about 1935. The maker must have been an accomplished seamstress, as the design of these plates is unusual and sophisticated. To begin, a quilter usually draws two concentric circles. The smaller inner circle forms the center; the outer one is divided into wedge shapes. This quilter divided the outer circle into twenty wedges and chose to do every fifth piece in a solid color as well as to cut its end as a point rather than as a curve. This slight variation on the traditional theme adds character and liveliness to a form which might otherwise seem somewhat pedestrian. The central portion of the plates is usually pieced as a simple circle, but this quilter chose to make a five-piece center which closely resembles the center of the Orange Peel pattern (see Chapter 9). The composition is framed with green wedge-shaped pieces, and the scalloped edge of the border repeats the scalloped edges of the plates, and the green used is the same shade as the solid green in each plate.

Variations on the Dresden Plate theme usually are no more significant than the number of wedges in the outer circle and the size of each motif. Plates with round edges are frequently found, others are scalloped like this one, and in some, all of the wedges are pointed. Usually the finished plates are appliquéd to a white ground (as has been done here), though occasionally a pastel background color is used. Less often the ground is pieced around the plates, and sometimes another motif, such as polka dots or small squares, may be interspersed between the plates. Since Dresden Plate requires careful piecing and sewing rounded edges, it is recommended for intermediate or advanced quilters.

Dresden Plate

SIZE: Approximately 65" x 102"

A mixture of pieced work and appliqué, the Dresden Plate design is relatively easy to recreate. We suggest that the quilter trace the full-size pattern pieces given on the opposite page, and then cut out templates in cardboard. The templates will assure the quilter that each piece cut from the fabric or fabrics used is of equal size. Be careful to allow ¼" for seams on all sides when cutting out the pieces.

This quilter made the sixteen "D" wedges of different plaid, striped, and calico cottons. The four "C" wedges (or spokes) are all of the same solid green color. Once the twenty wedge shapes are pieced together side to side, they are appliquéd onto the face of the quilt.

The quilt's unusual center can be completely pieced using one "A" and four "B" sections. Or four "B" sections can be appliquéd to the quilt. "A", then, is simply the exposed background.

All manner of borders have been used with this quilt pattern. The scalloped border shown here is particularly imaginative, but plainer borders and simple bindings can be just as effective.

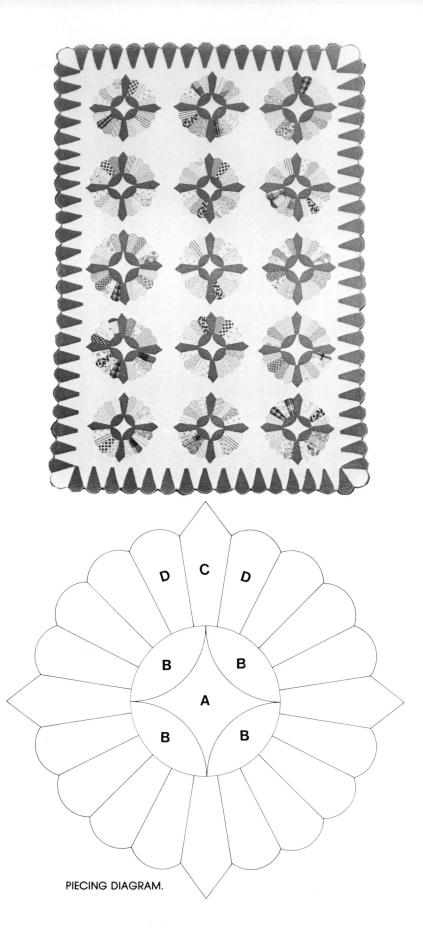

PIECING DIAGRAM.

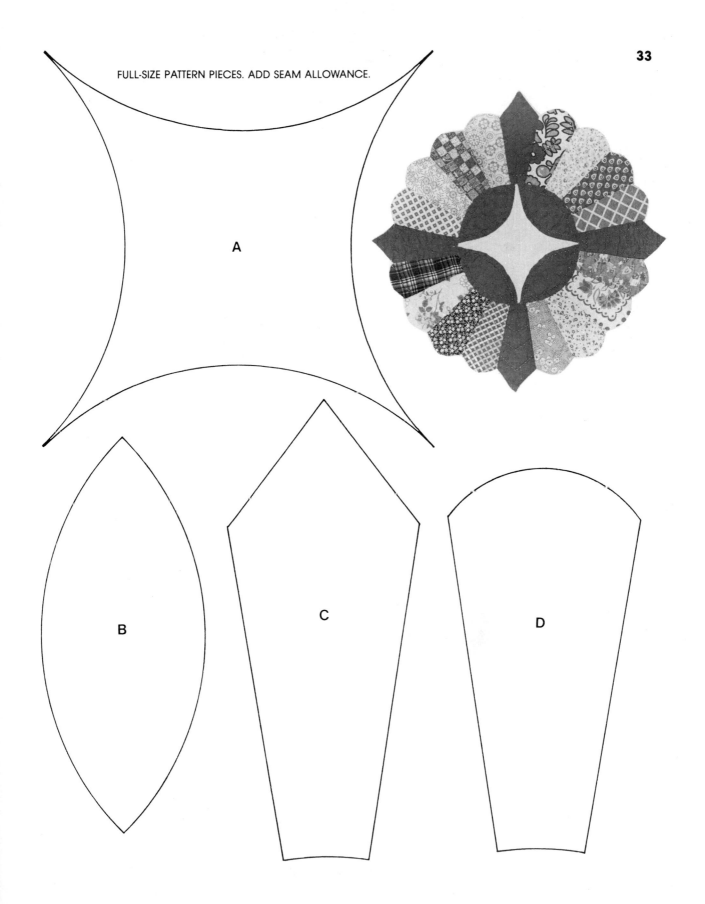

FULL-SIZE PATTERN PIECES. ADD SEAM ALLOWANCE.

A

B

C

D

7. Drunkard's Path

At first glance it seems hard to believe that this complicated-looking design, arranged to approximate the dizzying path of a drunkard heading home after a long night, is actually made from numerous simple two-patch pieces. A popular pattern since the late-19th century, Drunkard's Path has been called by many less Puritanical (if not as amusing) names: Country Husband, Fool's Puzzle, Pumpkin Vine, and Wonder of the World are just a few. The design has been made by quilters in all regions of America in every fabric from chintz to silk, cotton, wool, and linen. Although quilts of this design were generally intended for daily use (and were made for every bed size), numerous examples dating from the late 1800s and early 1900s have survived much wear and frequent laundering, and are available to the avid quilt collector today.

A wonderful pattern for the beginning quilter, Drunkard's Path is easily cut and pieced, though special attention must be paid to sewing the curves. Usually one dark and one light color are used—generally a deep red is set against white—though most any combination can be effective. In this case the pale blue striped fabric is set off beautifully by the stark white. To create the design, sixteen of the simple two-patch pieces—eight with the dark color as the larger piece, eight with the light—are placed edge to edge to create a large block. This process is repeated until the quilter has completed enough sixteen-piece blocks to make a quilt of the desired size. Then the large blocks are set side to side to complete the composition. Often large borders are added to allow space for quilting and to set off the finished piece. Borders and bindings of appropriate widths and colors can greatly enhance the charm of this design.

Drunkard's Path

SIZE: Approximately 71″ x 90½″

Despite the curves which must be sewn on each of the dozens of two-patches which go into the making of this quilt, Drunkard's Path is a fine pattern for the modern maker to recreate.

The best method of piecing the pattern is to make numerous blocks of sixteen two-patch pieces. (See piecing diagram.) When several of the large blocks have been completed, they may be pieced together to make the quilt. The desired effect of a weaving path is achieved by sewing eight of the two-patches with an "A" dark color piece and a "B" light color piece; the reverse color scheme is used for the other eight two-patches. When sixteen two-patches are completed, they are arranged in the manner shown in the piecing diagram.

The maker of the quilt illustrated here did not always sew her pattern pieces in the prescribed manner, and the careful observer will find numerous irregularities in this version of Drunkard's Path. The quilt has a 2 ³/₈″ wide, plain white, simply quilted border to frame the composition. A white binding ³/₈″ wide finishes the quilt.

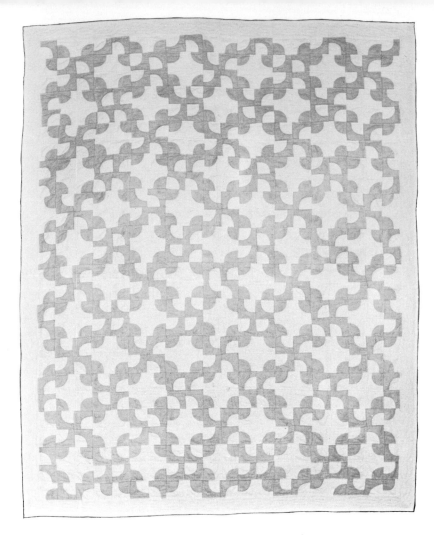

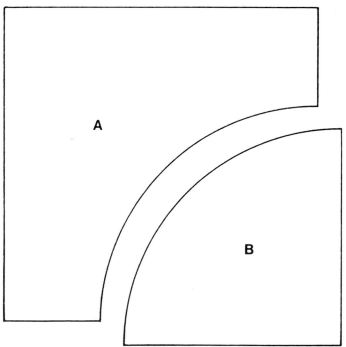

FULL-SIZE PIECING DIAGRAM.

ADD SEAM ALLOWANCE.

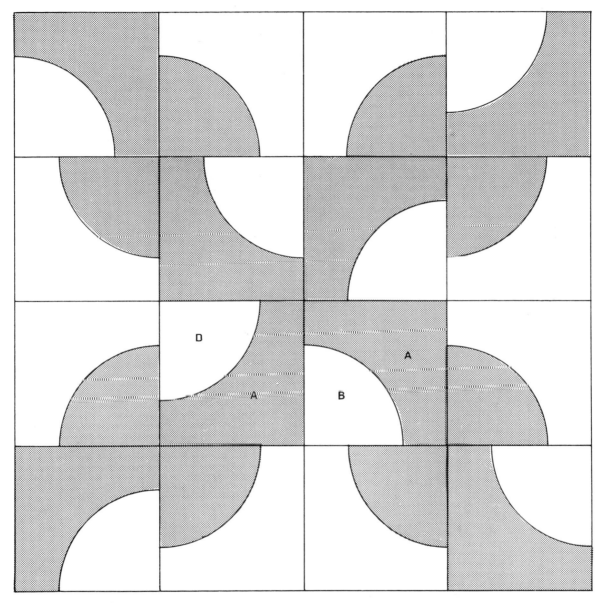

PIECING DIAGRAM.

8. Broken Star

ONE of the most dramatic and impressive of folk quilt patterns is the bold and graphic Broken Star design. A variation of the plainer Star of Bethlehem (see Chapter 28), the Broken Star pattern, evocative of a star exploding, adds force and movement to an already vibrant design.

The central star is pieced in much the same way as the Star of Bethlehem. Each of the eight central points is made separately, with thirty-six diamonds of equal size arranged in rows to form the large diamond shape. Once the star is completed, large squares of the field or background color (in this case white) are placed between the star points. Above each of the eight tips of the finished star, three new star points are placed. Ultimately, twenty-four points of the same color arrangement and dimensions (thirty-six equal pieces per point) make up the broken part of the star. Upon completion the image achieved is that of an eight-pointed star which has expanded into a sixteen-pointed star of a different style. The uninformed viewer may not realize that the entire composition is constructed of repeating elements of the same size and shape. To finish the quilt, large square patches and half-square patches of the background color are pieced between the outer star points; a binding or border may be added to frame the composition. The execution of this beautiful pattern should be undertaken only by advanced quilters, as extreme care must be taken in piecing all the elements. It is not uncommon to discover old Broken Star quilts lying discarded and unfinished in an attic trunk because the quilter could not correct the buckling of the pieces.

Popular from the mid-1800s onward, this striking pattern has been made by quilters throughout North America, though many of the most outstanding examples were executed in Pennsylvania. Due to the intricacy of the piecing and color arrangement, Broken Star quilts are generally quite large; many are about eighty inches square.

Dutch Rose or Carpenter's Wheel is a variant form with much the same visual effect, though it is far simpler to make. To produce this quilt, one begins with eight large diamond-shaped pieces which form the central star. Eight large square patches are fitted between the star points, and twenty-four diamond shapes of the same size as those in the central star are pieced around the outside to create the broken star effect. Though this pattern lacks the visual impact of the more complex version, it can be beautifully designed and is a fine piece for the advanced beginner or intermediate quilter.

Broken Star

SIZE: Approximately 82″ square

Difficult to piece because each of the tiny diamonds which make up the many points of the star must be cut and sewn exactly, this pattern is recommended only for experienced quilters.

The first step is to construct a series of thirty-two identical "C" pieces. Each of these pieces consists of thirty-six small diamonds (D). When finished, eight "C" pieces are sewn side to side to make the central star, and twenty-four "C" pieces are arranged to form the outer broken part of the star.

Next, 12″ x 12″ squares (A) are pieced between the inner star and the outer star. Three "A" pieces are also used in each of the four corners of the quilt.

To make the eight "B" pieces needed to finish the quilt, fold an "A" piece on the diagonal and cut it in half.

A wide border, commonly called for, has not been used in the illustrated example. Rather, the quilter chose to finish the quilt with a simple ¼″ binding.

The Carpenter's Wheel or Dutch Rose design is pieced in exactly the same way with the exception that the "C" form is cut from a single piece of fabric rather than being made up from thirty-six small diamonds.

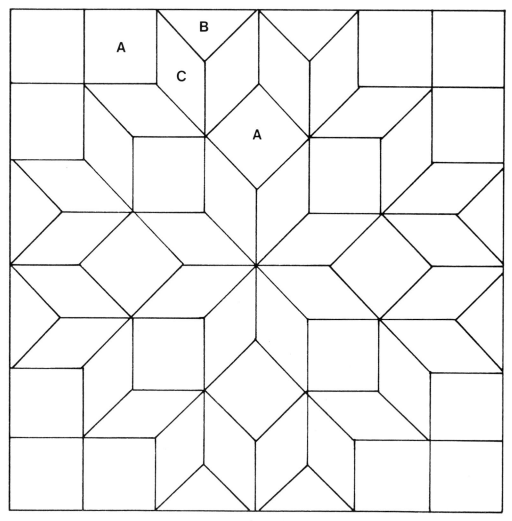

PIECING DIAGRAM.

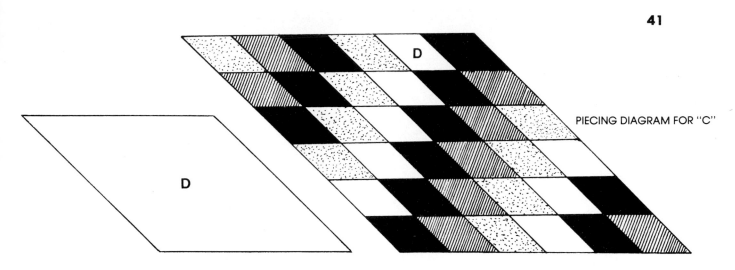

PIECING DIAGRAM FOR "C"

D

FULL-SIZE PATTERN PIECE. ADD SEAM ALLOWANCE.

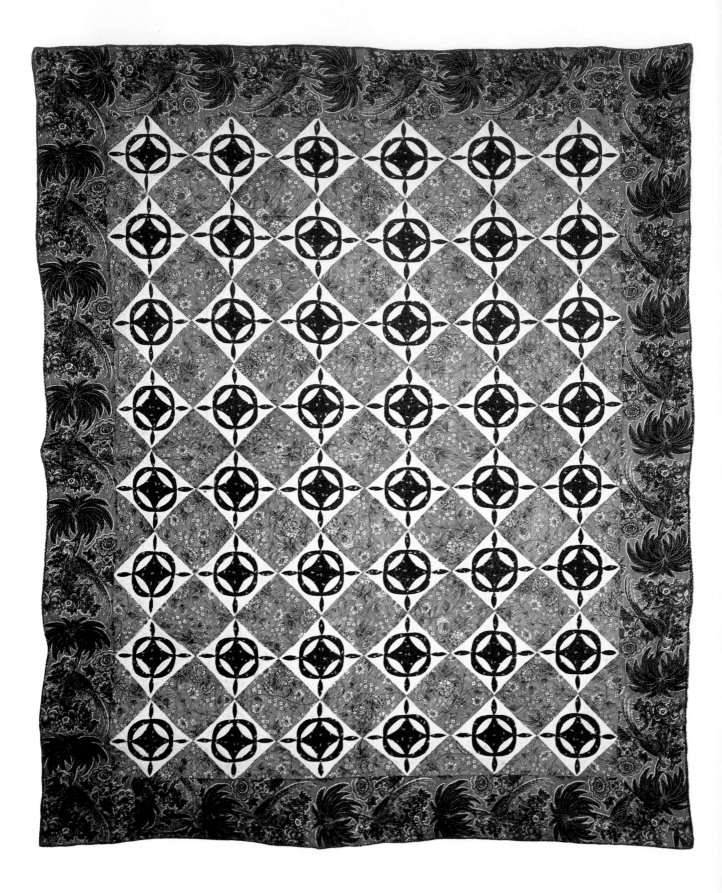

9. Orange Peel

A PATTERN which emerged in the late 18th century, Orange Peel was an excellent choice for the seamstress who was trying both to conserve fabric and to produce an integrated composition. To form the motif (which is known variously as Orange Peel, Reel, and Hickory Leaf), four oblong pieces are cut out of the central circle and then are reused as the points which reach into the four corners of the graphic patches. The empty spaces are filled in with a complementary shade; in the illustrated example the reel is green and the background is white.

Made in Bergen County, New Jersey, in the first quarter of the 19th century, this quilt is a particularly fine example of the Orange Peel design. The imaginative maker combined three different roller-printed chintz patterns to achieve a wonderfully decorative effect. Roller printed chintzes were fashionable at that time, and they could be found in all manner of designs and colors. The dark green and white graphic patches are elegantly offset by the blue and pink floral pattern in the alternating squares. The unusual border pattern, with its palm trees, peacocks, and fantastic flowers, is an interesting alternative to a plain quilted border. It adds continuity to the composition by echoing the green of the reel and the blue of the alternating squares. A plain border framing these complicated and vivid patches would have been far less effective.

Many less sophisticated color combinations have been used in the piecing of this pattern. Cotton solids, calicoes, and prints were most commonly employed because of their availability and reasonable price, but quilts of chintz, wool, and silk are found occasionally today. Probably because of the many curved pieces in this pattern, Orange Peel was not produced as regularly as other folk quilt designs, yet the experienced quilter should find this an exceptionally pleasing pattern to recreate.

Orange Peel

SIZE: Approximately 78″ x 98″

Considered a difficult quilt to piece because of the many curves in the central motif, Orange Peel is recommended for experienced quilters. To recreate this design, the maker produces forty-eight 7″ x 7″ theme blocks.

The reel motif can be pieced or appliquéd; appliqué is by far the easier method. The center piece (A) and the four petal tips (C) can be cut from a single circular piece of fabric.

FULL-SIZE PIECING DIAGRAM. ADD SEAM ALLOWANCE.

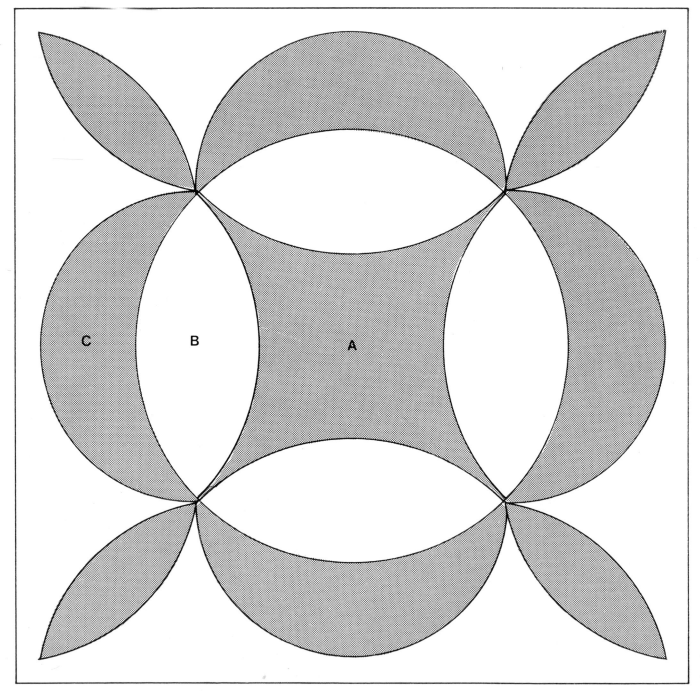

The circle is folded in half, and two pieces are cut from the curved side. The oval pieces, with seams turned under, form four perfect petals. The curved pieces (B) can all be cut at once from four pieces of fabric. Don't forget to leave room for the seams!

Once finished, the graphic squares are set on the diagonal and arranged tip to tip. Plain squares (also 7" x 7") of the background fabric are pieced between the graphic patches.

To finish the central area, half-square pieces (D) are placed between the theme blocks. Smaller triangles (E) are sewn in the four corners. The border is 8½" wide, and a ½" binding finishes the composition.

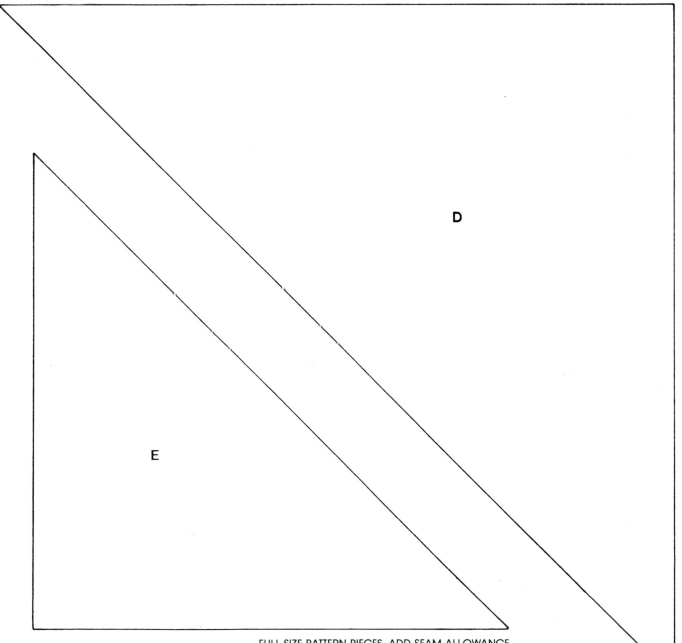

D

E

FULL-SIZE PATTERN PIECES. ADD SEAM ALLOWANCE.

10. Triple Irish Chain

ONE of the oldest of quilt patterns, the Triple Irish Chain has long been popular among quilters for the simplicity of its pattern and the large open areas it provides for the practice of quilting techniques. Irish chains are made in three basic ways: the simplest is the Single Irish Chain, consisting of single chains of small squares turned on the diagonal which cross the face of the quilt. The Double Irish Chain is composed of chains three blocks wide, the central one being generally of a lighter color. The Triple Irish Chain is five blocks wide and is usually pieced in three different colors and white or in a variety of calicoes or printed fabrics. As Irish Chain quilts were most often made for everyday use, many quilters did not treat them as showpieces, but instead took advantage of the opportunity to use up tiny scraps of fabric, a practice which has produced a wonderful variety of color combinations.

Although the construction appears to be quite complex, it is, in fact, relatively easy. The design is made up of two different types of patches of forty-nine squares each which are then pieced together to form the continuous chains. (See diagrams on the following pages). Traditionally each square measures one by one inch. Many quilters use random colors or calico prints in the making of each chain, though more elegant effects can be achieved through careful color strategies. A Triple Irish Chain quilt looks most captivating when a light central chain is used and two harmonious colors are chosen for the four outer chains. As in the example illustrated, the design can be enhanced by the addition of matching borders and binding.

As these quilts are often made of odds and ends, it is most common to find examples in solid cottons or cotton calicoes, although rare woolen, silk, and linsey-woolsey examples do exist. Because this pattern has been popular since the beginning of the 1800s (and was made even earlier), the range of roller prints, prints, calicoes, and solids found in antique examples is as wide as the types of material that were available to the quilter.

One of the most pleasing variations of the Irish Chain pattern produced over the years is a design called Burgoyne Surrounded. Name for a British Revolutionary War general who was forced to surrender to the Americans at Saratoga, the pattern is said to be based on the actual military deployment which led to his capture. Other variations of the Irish Chain include Puss in the Corner and Double Nine-Patch.

Triple Irish Chain

SIZE: Approximately 81″ square

Though the Triple Irish Chain pattern may seem overwhelming at first glance, it is really quite easy to construct. Made of numerous 2″ squares, it is, however, time-consuming to piece.

Two block types (A and B) are necessary to form this design. Each of the blocks is 14″ square. "A" is made with twelve 2″ squares of two colors (in this case, eight blue and four red) which are pieced or appliquéd in the corners of a plain piece of fabric. (See diagram.) The empty area in the center is usually quilted.

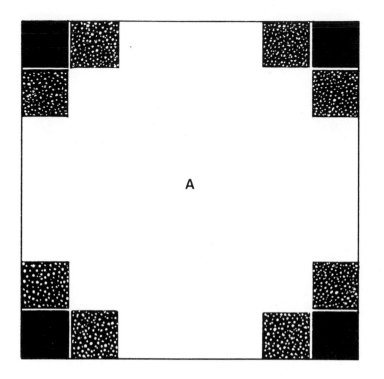

PIECING DIAGRAMS.

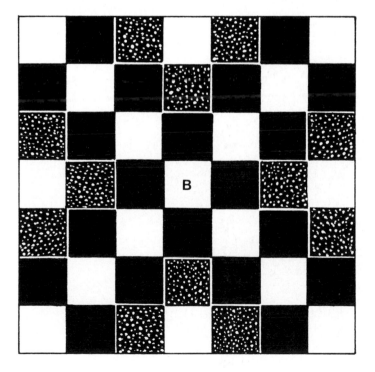

"B" is made from forty-nine 2″ squares of four colors (in this case, yellow, red, blue, and white). In the piecing diagrams "A" and "B", red is represented by black squares, yellow by gray, and blue by speckled. Twelve "A" and thirteen "B" blocks are needed to piece the graphic area of this quilt.

This maker added three borders of equal width (1¾″) to the outer edges of the composition. The binding is ⅝″ wide. A single border with a contrasting binding can be just as effective as this design.

B	A	B	A	B
A	B	A	B	A
B	A	B	A	B
A	B	A	B	A
B	A	B	A	B

One of the oldest of quilt patterns, Triple Irish Chain has been made in countless color combinations; modern quilters may want to attempt original schemes of their own. Before beginning, plot out the design on graph paper so that you will have some idea how the finished product will look in advance.

11. Flying Geese

TWICE each year flocks of geese migrating to summer or winter quarters make their journey across the skies. The image of these birds in flight has always been captivating, and it is not surprising to find the theme of flying geese represented in one of the oldest and most appealing of quilt patterns. A classic geometric design formed of crisp lines and firmly delineated angles, Flying Geese is as appropriate in a sleek contemporary setting as in the rustic cabins in which it was first made and used.

Easy to piece, the Flying Geese pattern is perfect for the novice quilter. Each "goose" is formed of an identical isosceles triangle. Two smaller triangles, usually of white to provide the greatest contrast, form the end pieces which are attached to each "goose". The geese are added one to another to produce a strip of the desired length. Strips of geese are divided by plain strips, generally of another color, until the required width is reached. Often the rows of geese are made in alternating light and dark hues. Color choice is crucial: the geese may be done in different calicoes or scraps, but generally the best effect is achieved when variety is limited to different shades of one or two colors. Usually the quilt is finished by a simple binding or plain border, but on occasion bars of flying geese have been used to frame the entire composition.

The precise origin of this quilt pattern is unknown, but examples have been produced in the East and Midwest since the times of the early settlers, and are found in every fabric from cotton to silk. In the first half of the 19th century, fine roller-printed cottons and chintzes were often used for the bars between the rows of geese.

The Flying Geese pattern is also known as Flocks of Birds, Ocean Waves, and Birds in the Air. There are several variants of this simple form including a pattern where the bars cross the face of the quilt on the diagonal. In some cases the bars start on opposite sides of the composition and cross each other in the middle of the field. A more complicated variant of the Flying Geese pattern, known as Wild Goose Chase, is described at length in Chapter 12.

52

Flying Geese

Sɪᴢᴇ: Approximately 95″ square.

An old and time-tested pattern, Flying Geese is easy to piece and the finished quilt adds a joyous touch to any room.

The dimensions supplied here are slightly different from those of the original quilt, but the revised size is easier to cut and piece; the quilt will make a spread for a queen-size bed. Nine strips of geese should alternate with ten plain strips. The plain strips are done in red calico; the geese are worked in varying shades of brown calico. The red calico border at the top and bottom of the quilt is 2¾″ wide; the binding which finishes the composition is ⅜″.

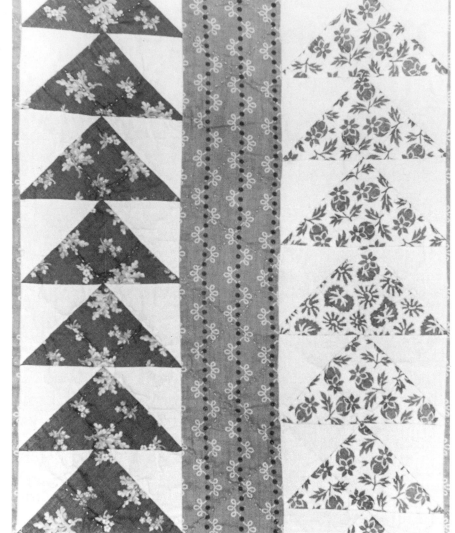

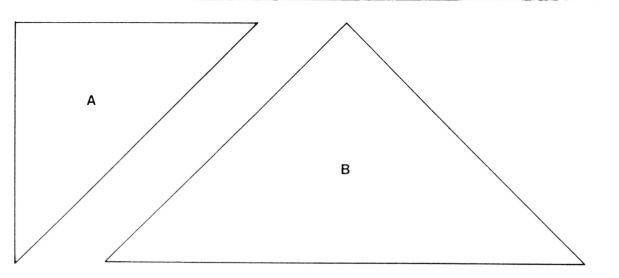

FULL-SIZE PATTERN PIECES. ADD SEAM ALLOWANCE.

In the pattern recommended here, both the strips of geese and the plain strips are 5″ wide. The strips of geese are thirty-six geese long. The quilter who wishes to change the dimensions of this quilt can do so quite easily by adding to or subtracting from the length of the strips and by changing the number of plain and graphic strips which make up the field of this quilt.

Only two pattern pieces (A,B) are required for this design. When cutting, be sure to leave ¼″ extra on all sides of the pieces for the seam allowance. The small end triangles (B) which fit between the geese (A) are usually pieced in white as white provides the best contrast.

The Flying Geese pattern may be used to provide interesting borders for other, more complicated patterns, or it can be made to serve as the backing for another quilt, rendering the blanket reversible.

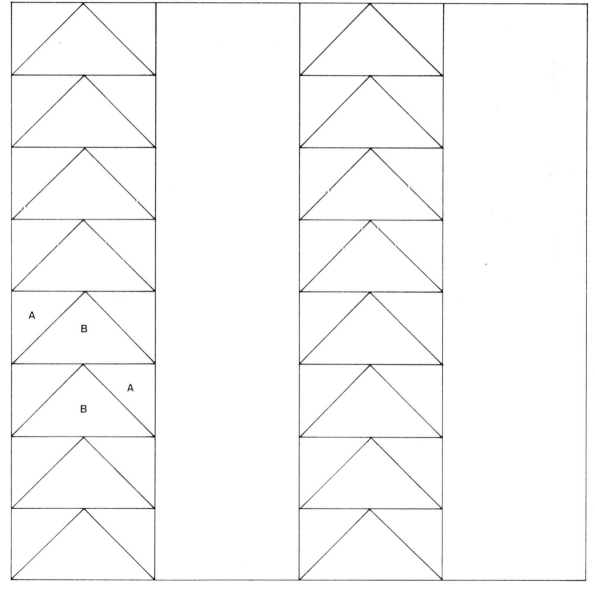

PIECING DIAGRAM.

12. Wild Goose Chase

WILD Goose Chase is one of many variations on an early pieced quilt pattern—Flying Geese—and has been popular since the early-19th century with Amish and Mennonite quilters as well as with others outside those communities. The pattern has been pieced in every size and type of fabric, though, since these quilts were created largely for daily use, cotton is the prevalent material found in antique examples.

This lovely quilt of raspberry and olive green was made in Cumberland County, Pennsylvania, by the same woman—Mrs. Giegle—who pieced Fox and Geese (Chapter 23). She must have found the triangular "geese" especially appealing to work with. In this example, the graphic patches show geese flying in all directions rather than in straight lines as in Flying Geese (Chapter 11). Mrs. Giegle chose to form her quilt out of twelve identically-pieced blocks (three across and four down) separated by a two-color grid. The blocks are relatively easy to piece: five isosceles triangles which are the "geese" emanate in four directions from a central square. End triangles in a contrasting color are placed between the geese. In the corner of each block is a square either in a contrasting color or in the same color as the geese. The areas between the rows of geese are filled in with large triangles of the background color. The wide mauve border serves to soften the bright raspberry of the grid. Working in the 1880s, Mrs. Giegle was probably limited in her choice of fabrics, and the "geese" do not always stand out well against the background. The modern quilter may want to use bolder colors to heighten the sense of movement which can be imparted by this vibrant pattern.

Changes in the position and number of the Wild Goose Chase patches can substantially alter the quilt's effect. One alternative would be to turn the blocks on the axis, thus giving them the appearance of diamonds. When this is done, the bands of geese fly toward the four points of the compass. Another variation would be to alternate plain blocks with graphic ones. The grid can also be eliminated or altered. The most dramatic option uses pieced bands of flying geese for the grid and the border.

Aside from Flying Geese and Fox and Geese, there are numerous designs which draw on the idea of birds in flight and in which the creatures are represented by isosceles triangles. Among them are Flock of Birds, Birds in Flight, Birds in the Air, Goose in the Pond, Ducks and Ducklings, and Hens and Chickens.

Wild Goose Chase

SIZE: Approximately 61″ x 67″

The "geese" motif in Wild Goose Chase is pieced in much the same manner as Flying Geese (Chapter 11). The strips of geese should be made first and then the other elements added to form the blocks. (The original quilt shown on p. 54 has five geese in each strip. These have been reduced in number to make piecing simpler.) The four strips of geese in each graphic block should consist of four colored geese (B) and six end triangles of a contrasting color (in this case, white). At the end of the strip are placed two white "B" triangles and an "A" square. The finished strips are then attached to the central diamond which consists of an "A" square to which four "C" triangles have been attached. The large "D" triangles are pieced between the strips of geese. Each of the twelve graphic blocks are 10½″ square.

To make the grid between the blocks, thirty-one 10½″ x 3″ "E" pieces and twenty 3″ x 3″ "F" pieces are required. The grid looks best if "E" and "F" are of contrasting colors.

This quilter chose to make the border 8½″ wide on the sides and 5″ wide on top and bottom. A narrow ⅜″ binding surrounds the entire composition.

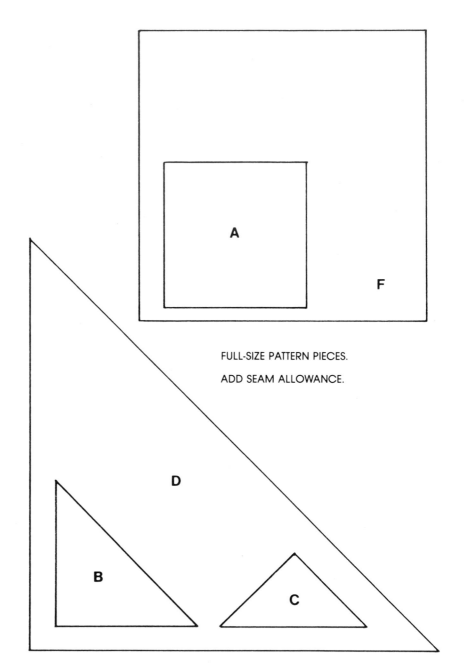

FULL-SIZE PATTERN PIECES.

ADD SEAM ALLOWANCE.

PIECING DIAGRAM.

13. Bear's Paw

THIS vivid and striking quilt, constructed in fabrics of vibrant blue and purple and edged with a complementary shade of brown, provides a fine example of the marvelous color sense of the Amish. It was sewn by an Ohio Amish quilter or quilters around 1910. The name "Bear's Paw" refers to the wild creature which was once frequently encountered in the area where the quilt was made; Bear's Paw has been the traditional name for several patterns worked by quilters in Western Pennsylvania and Ohio at a time when bear tracks were commonly seen.

On Long Island, where the wildlife is less ferocious, the same basic pattern was often called Duck's Foot in the Mud. In Philadelphia, Quaker designs of this type are known as Hands of Friendship, and in Southern states, where square dancing is common, the pattern and its variants are named Hands All Around. Very popular in the late-19th century and again in the 1920s and '30s, especially among the Amish, Bear's Paw quilts have been constructed in a variety of fabrics including wool, cotton, and silk.

Though the pattern on the opposite page is a variant of a better known Bear's Paw design, it is easy to piece and ideal for the beginning quilter. Essentially this quilt may be thought of as a nine-patch consisting of two different four-patch types—one made of four squares, the other of four triangles—with a plain square set in the middle. Thirteen Bear's Paw patches alternate with twelve solid patches which are pieced in offset rows. The composition is framed by a deep blue border surrounded by a wider border of the same shade as the purple used in the nine-patches. The outer border is the same color as the backing—a design detail which serves to integrate the composition.

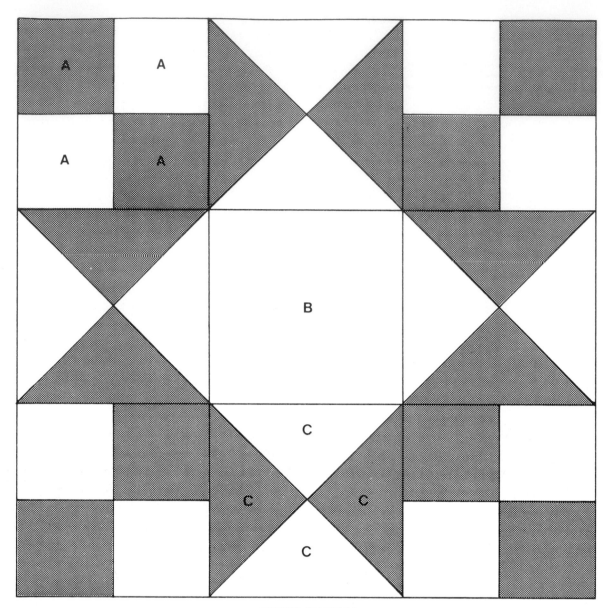

A A

A A

B

C

C C

C

PIECING DIAGRAM.

Bear's Paw

SIZE: Approximately 70″ square

A variation of the straight-forward Nine-Patch pattern, Bear's Paw is an easy and extremely pleasing pattern to recreate. Each of the thirteen 9″ x 9″ graphic patches is made up from eight 3″ x 3″ four-patch pieces and a single plain 3″ square.

There are two types of four-patch blocks used: one is constructed of four 1½″ squares (A); the second is made of four triangles with 3″ bases (C). To achieve the Bear's Paw effect, it is essential to use two contrasting colors and to piece them as indicated in the diagram (above). Four of each of the two types of four-patches are required to make each Bear's Paw patch.

To begin, the quilter should trace the full-size pattern pieces drawn here and then cut out templates in cardboard. The ¼″ seam allowances may be added before cutting the templates or they may be added when cutting the fabric.

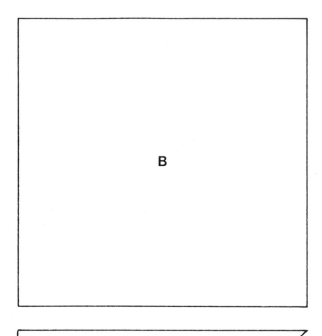

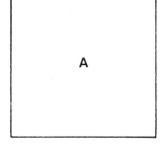

B

A

FULL-SIZE PATTERN PIECES.
ADD SEAM ALLOWANCE.

C

Thirteen graphic patches alternate with twelve plain patches. The small inner border is 3½″ wide; the outer border is 7½″. A rather wide binding is called for, this one being 1¼″ across.

14. Feathered Star

THE star has long been one of the most popular of quilt motifs and has been pieced in many imaginatively-named patterns. The Feathered Star is known variously as Twinkling Star and Sawtooth Star. It can be composed of either one large central star or a group of smaller ones. Frequently the stars are found within a pieced grid; sometimes a sawtooth border surrounds the composition; and often (as in the quilt illustrated here) there is simply a narrow binding.

To create a single Feathered Star, the quilter begins with a plain central block to which eight smaller triangles (squares cut on the diagonal) are attached. These "half-squares" form the bases of the star points or rays. Smaller half-squares and squares are added to the outer edges of the eight star points to create a feathered appearance. At the tip of each point is placed a diamond-shaped patch which completes each of the rays. The size of each patch will range from tiny to very large depending upon the number of stars included in the design and the overall size of the quilt. A more complicated pattern than it might at first seem, Feathered Star should only be attempted by advanced quilters.

Cotton has always been the preferred medium for this design, though woolen examples can be found. The quilt depicted on the opposite page was made with an indigo blue calico which was set against a white ground, but often quilters choose different colors for the points, feathers, and central block, and colors may vary from star to star within the same quilt.

Both old and new examples of this vibrant pattern are found in almost all areas of North America in almost every shape and size: crib, trundle, single, 3/4, full, and very large quilts made for 19th-century poster beds are represented in collections throughout America.

Both simpler and more complex versions of the basic Feathered Star pattern (central square surrounded by smaller half-squares) can be constructed. Slight changes in the piecing of the central block will give the quilt a new name: if it is made with a nine-patch in the center of each star it becomes a California Star; with a central hexagon it is known as a Radiant Star. The Variable Star pattern (see Chapter 3) is another design of the same type—it is created by simply eliminating the "feathers" and the diamonds from the outer edges of the eight points.

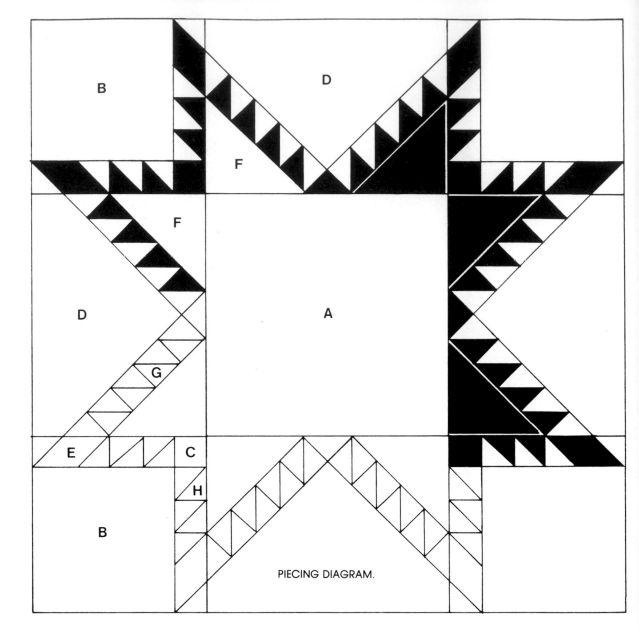

B

D

F

F

D

A

G

E   C

H

B

PIECING DIAGRAM.

Feathered Star

SIZE: Approximately 75″
square

Though it is widely agreed that
this bold and graphic design is
one of the most difficult of
traditional patterns to piece, it
is also one of the most appealing to undertake. It is suggested
that the quilter trying this pattern for the first time cut and
piece a sample block before
undertaking such a large, complex project.

Try to see the piecing diagram
(above) as a complicated version of the Nine-Patch. This
will help in the making of the
quilt, as the patches can be accomplished one by one and
then sewed together. The difficulty is not in the sewing, for
all the pieces are joined along
straight lines; problems may
arise if all the little "feathers"
are not exactly the same size. If
they are not, the star will not
lie flat.

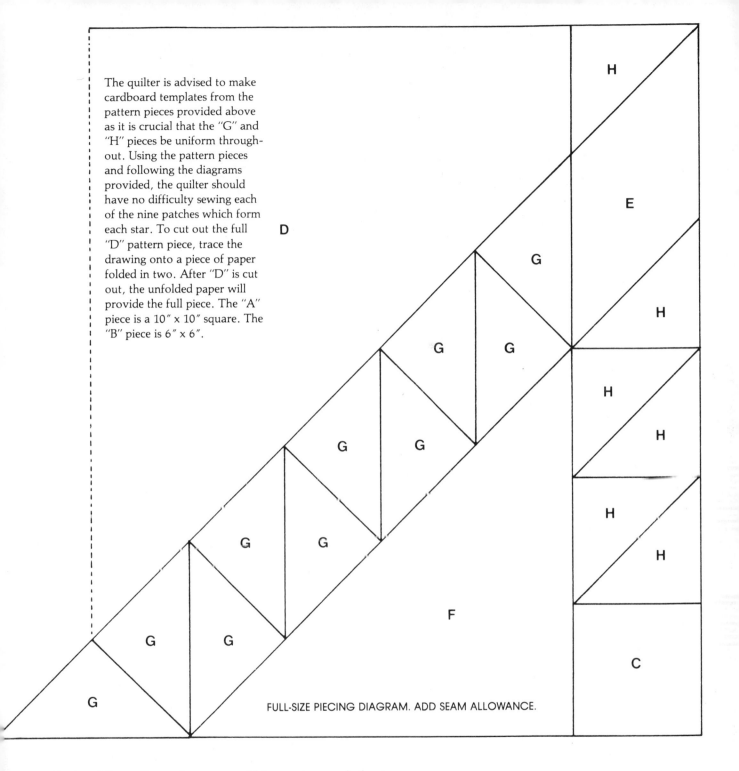

The quilter is advised to make cardboard templates from the pattern pieces provided above as it is crucial that the "G" and "H" pieces be uniform throughout. Using the pattern pieces and following the diagrams provided, the quilter should have no difficulty sewing each of the nine patches which form each star. To cut out the full "D" pattern piece, trace the drawing onto a piece of paper folded in two. After "D" is cut out, the unfolded paper will provide the full piece. The "A" piece is a 10" x 10" square. The "B" piece is 6" x 6".

FULL-SIZE PIECING DIAGRAM. ADD SEAM ALLOWANCE.

Feathered Star quilts can be made in numerous styles. A pieced grid sewn between each of the stars is one attractive design alternative.

This seamstress made the stars of the same color, but the modern quilter may prefer a more colorful scheme. She also preferred a plain narrow binding to a more ornate border and binding combination.

65

15. Trip Around the World

THE delicate subtly-toned composition illustrated on the opposite page was made by an Iowa quilter in the 1930s. Pastels were popular during that period, but scraps must have been saved for years before this piece was attempted. The careful observer will note that each of the thirty-seven rows of one-inch squares is constructed of a different fabric. Only through careful planning and arrangement of the shades of these solid, calico, and striped materials was the quilter able to achieve this delightful, almost kaleidoscopic effect. The colors are reminiscent of a wedding: perhaps this quilt was made by a mother in celebration of her daughter's marriage.

Though extremely time-consuming, the construction of Trip Around the World is not complicated. A variation of the most basic of all quilt designs, the one-patch, Trip Around the World is formed by concentric squares which are pieced together from the center out. Usually there is only one central square—in this case there are three—and the squares may be set end to end, rather than diagonally from point to point as they are in this case. Setting the squares on the axis generally creates a more sophisticated-looking result.

Trip Around the World is also known as Philadelphia Pavement, and the name is often used interchangeably with Sunshine and Shadow (see Chapter 26). Frequently, however, the name Trip Around the World refers to quilts made by those outside the Amish and Mennonite communities; the worldly examples do not have the wide, beautifully-quilted borders which are the hallmarks of Amish pieces. Instead the outer row finishes the quilt, and may, as in the example illustrated here, be the same color as the backing.

Trip Around the World became popular in the mid-19th century, and early examples may be found in wool, cotton, and silk. When American women rediscovered quilting in the late '20s and '30s, Trip Around the World became popular once again. As the pattern has been considered an easy one for the advanced beginner or intermediate-level quilter, antique examples are found with some frequency.

Trip Around the World

Sɪᴢᴇ: Approximately 108″ x 117″

A variation of the simple one-patch, Trip Around the World is made of numerous 1½″ squares. To recreate this version of the classic pattern, the quilter begins with three central squares set on the diagonal. To these are sewn eight squares of another shade, then twelve more of yet another hue, then sixteen, and so on. In this case, the thirty-seventh and outermost concentric rectangle consists of 150 squares.

Another alternative is to start Trip Around the World with only one central square. The squares also may be set straight rather than on the axis, though the latter choice seems to add liveliness and energy to the pattern.

COLOR KEY   PIECING DIAGRAM.

 solid pink

pink and white calico

 pink, purple, and white calico

bright yellow and pink calico

blue and white calico

blue, pink, and white calico

 solid blue

 blue windowpane checks

A straightforward and lovely pattern, Trip Around the World depends upon careful color planning to achieve the optimum dramatic effect. The color key (at left) corresponds to the piecing diagram above and makes use of the colors originally chosen by the seamstress who made the illustrated example.

This quilter made thirty-seven concentric rectangles, each one of a different printed or solid cotton. Though she often used several bands of the same color, the shades and prints always vary at least slightly. The modern quilter may prefer to repeat a series of standard colors. One could follow the key indicated here and repeat each of the eight colors indicated four or five times. Naturally, there are limitless possibilities. The essential thing is to plan first.

16. Double Wedding Ring

A PLEASING pattern which has been employed thousands of times to make countless wedding presents, Double Wedding Ring is formed from interlocking circles which symbolize the bond of marriage and the rings exchanged by husband and wife. Though this pattern was first produced in the mid-19th century, it did not reach the height of its popularity until the early 1900s. It is a difficult pattern to piece, but the introduction of pre-cut templates and even pre-cut pattern pieces in the 20th century has rendered the work much easier. The quilt illustrated here was made in eastern Jefferson County, Kentucky, in 1924 by Mary Gering. She may have used a quilt kit as the pieces are all of exactly the right size and the distribution of color and fabrics is precisely the same from ring to ring. Dresden Plate (Chapter 6), the other highly popular design of the early 1900s, was also widely available in kit form. Many periodicals of the day published patterns and instructions for piecing these quilts.

Double Wedding Ring has been made in all 20th-century bed sizes from king to twin and is occasionally found in matching pairs. Usually pieced of cotton, the pattern continues to be a favorite of quilters in every area of North America, perhaps because of the rings' romantic symbolism. Examples made by Amish or Mennonite quilters have been found, but generally these are pieced in strong colors rather than in pastels.

The pattern's full field and rather complicated design leave little room for variation. The interlocking rings, scalloped border, and thin binding are standard elements. Quilts of this design with wide borders are rarely found. Amish and Mennonite examples, however, often have straight rather than scalloped borders. The one well-known variation of the design is Indian Wedding Ring. It differs in the use of triangular pieces rather than wedges in the circular bands; the areas enclosed by the bands are pieced in a fabric that contrasts in color with the field. Both Double Wedding Ring and Indian Wedding Ring are relatively difficult designs to cut and piece as they require the sewing of curved lines. Even experienced quilters will find them a challenge.

Double Wedding Ring

Size: Approximately 95″ x 110″

Very difficult to sew because of the small size and curved edges of the numerous pattern pieces in each ring, Double Wedding Ring is suitable only for experienced quilters. Before starting to cut, the maker should make cardboard templates of the pattern pieces (A, B, C). When cutting, add ¼″ on all sides for the seam allowance. Be sure to cut and sew precisely or the rings will not fit together.

To begin piecing, the maker sews together four "A" pieces of the appropriate colors (see color key) and then adds a "B" piece to both ends. A green or purple "C" piece is then sewn at one end. (Half of the 194 strips necessary to recreate this quilt have green pieces on one end; half have purple). Then the process is repeated, reversing the order of the colors (see key) but with the same color "C" piece at the opposite end. The curved strips are joined to make a football-shape piece. Ninety-seven of these oval shapes are needed to complete the quilt.

The ovals are then appliquéd to the background fabric which is usually white. All of the ovals with purple "C" pieces on both ends should be placed horizontally across the face of the quilt; those with green pieces should be placed vertically. There are eight horizontal rows which are six ovals across, and seven vertical rows seven ovals long.

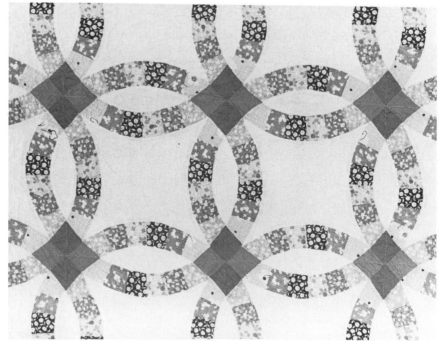

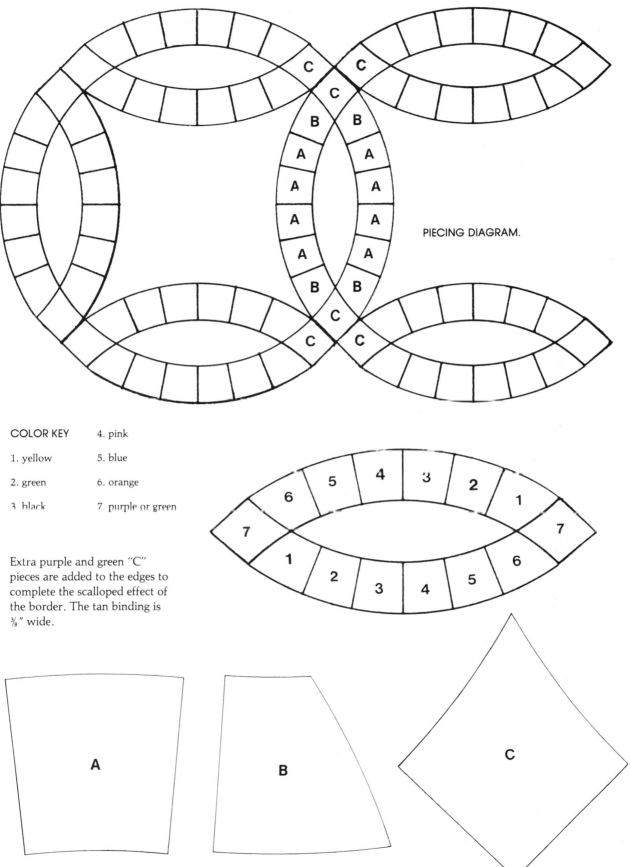

PIECING DIAGRAM.

COLOR KEY

1. yellow
2. green
3. black
4. pink
5. blue
6. orange
7. purple or green

Extra purple and green "C" pieces are added to the edges to complete the scalloped effect of the border. The tan binding is ⅜" wide.

FULL-SIZE PATTERN PIECES. ADD SEAM ALLOWANCE.

17. Tree of Life

COLONISTS on the Eastern seaboard began to produce Tree of Life quilts during the 17th century. It is thought that the basic pattern was adapted from needlework designs. Whatever the origin of the motif, a tree of this sort, which resembles a pine, was a particularly appropriate symbol to the early settlers. Pine trees grew in abundance, and they were literally necessities of life, providing logs for cabins and barns, furniture for interiors, and firewood for cooking and warmth. Colonial Americans paid tribute to the pine on coins and flags, and it is not surprising to find the theme translated into a quilt pattern.

Popularity of the Tree of Life pattern spread throughout North America during the 19th century as the pioneers pushed West. It has been used on quilts of all sizes and made with all available fabrics. Wool, chintz, and silk examples can be found, though cotton calicoes, prints, and solids are far more common. The Amish and Mennonites produced many fine examples of this pattern in the late 1800s and in the 1920s and '30s. The design is also known as Christmas Tree, Temperance Tree, Tall Pine Tree, Tree of Paradise, and Tree of Temptation.

Though the pine tree blocks of the quilt shown here are constructed entirely of geometric pieces which are sewed along straight lines, the large number of small triangles used for each graphic patch requires the skilled piecing ability of an intermediate or advanced quilter. The branch and needle parts of the tree are made up entirely of half-squares of contrasting colors. The trunk is composed of a long arrow-shaped piece; the base consists of two triangles. Three triangles and two five-sided pieces of the background color (in this case, white) are pieced to the tree form. In the illustrated example, made in New Jersey circa 1850, each of the trees is separated by a grid in the same color as the field. The overall composition is framed in the same green calico used for the tree trunks.

There are, however, other variations on the Tree of Life theme. Some quilts consist of a single large pine tree rather than numerous small ones; in others, the tree or trees are shaped differently than shown here. In some Tree of Life quilts, graphic patches alternate with plain ones and the grid between the patches is of a contrasting color. In most cases, the border is quite wide and affords space for intricate quilting.

Tree of Life

SIZE: Approximately 83″ x 91″

This lovely pattern is easier to piece than it would first appear, but special care must be taken to cut each of the individual pieces correctly. It is suggested that the quilter make cardboard templates before beginning. Don't forget to leave enough extra fabric for making the seams. Usually, ¼″ is enough.

Within each of the 12″ graphic blocks are fifty-four "C" half-squares and three "F" squares which represent the foliage. The trunk, usually of another color, is constructed of two "C" half-squares, one "B" half-square, and a large "D" piece. The background, which is generally white, is made from two "E" pieces (one reversed), one "B" piece, and two "A" pieces.

This quilter used twenty-two graphic patches and separated them with a grid. The grid is formed from "G" and "H" pieces which are 3″ square and 12″ x 3″, respectively. Instead of using a grid to separate the trees, other quilters have chosen to alternate graphic patches with plain patches.

An exact recreation of this quilt should have a border 2⅜″ wide and a binding ⅜″ wide. The modern quilter, however, may try new ways of finishing the Tree of Life quilt.

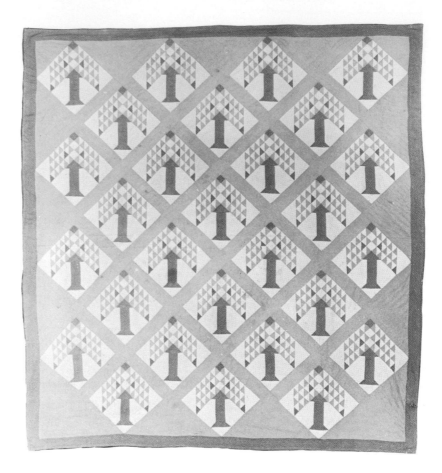

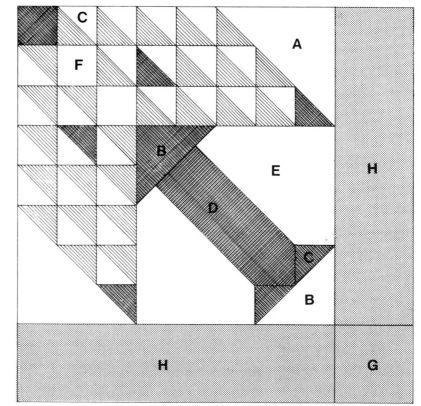

PIECING DIAGRAM.

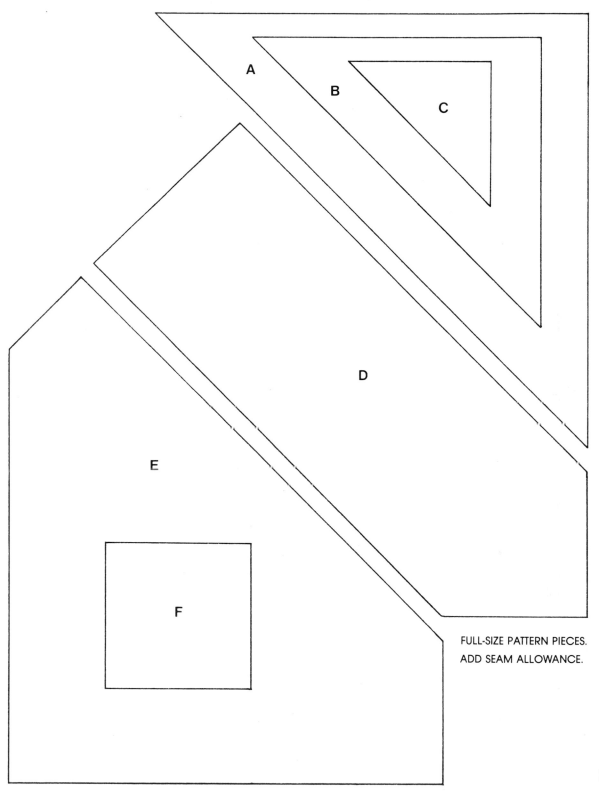

A

B

C

D

E

F

FULL-SIZE PATTERN PIECES.
ADD SEAM ALLOWANCE.

18. Houses

For those who prefer representational designs to abstract ones, Houses is one of the more appealing patterns to recreate. First made in the mid-19th century, probably in New Jersey, House or Schoolhouse quilts are usually made up of solid colored fabrics—frequently red buildings are placed against a white ground—though multi-colored calicoes and stripes are sometimes seen. Most early examples of this quilt design were made in the East; examples from the Midwest date from the late-19th century.

The method of construction of this pattern varies from example to example: in some the houses are completely pieced (as in the quilt illustrated here), others are pieced and appliquéd, and some are entirely appliquéd. Though they may be put together differently, the basic shape of the structures depicted remains the same from quilt to quilt regardless of whether they are called houses, cottages, schoolhouses, barns, or churches: generally a side wall and one end of the house are shown. Sometimes a cupola, steeple, silo, or belltower identifies the building, but most often the houses are capped with simple chimneys. Occasionally, the house theme is used to build compositions which illustrate whole neighborhoods or towns, and a variety of different buildings appears on the field. Quilts of this design are unusual, however, and can be visually confusing.

Placement of the houses on the field of the quilt is crucial to the overall design. Often a grid is used to separate the houses one from another; sometimes they are simply arranged in straight rows with the bases of the houses parallel to the bottom of the quilt. They also may be arranged as they are here. To the viewer standing on one side of the bed, half of the rows of houses appear to be upside down. The framing of the composition varies with this pattern. Wide borders of a solid fabric can be as effective as a simple binding or a more complicated design.

Houses

Size: Approximately 77″ square.

Houses has been a favorite pattern of quilters over the years, and quilts made from this design may be pieced or appliquéd. The example illustrated here is completely pieced, but the pattern pieces given are for appliqué. If the modern quilter prefers to piece the quilt rather than appliqué, the background pieces necessary can be easily deduced from the pattern pieces given.

This square single-bed size quilt was made from thirty-six houses arranged in six rows. Two inches of fabric are allowed between the sides of each house and between the rows of houses. There is 1″ between the houses and the border. The triangles in the inner border each have a 2″ base and 1½″ sides. The outer border is 2¼″ wide; the binding is ⅜″ wide.

The houses are pieced as indicated by the diagram. The roof and side wall of the house are placed ½″ apart as are the front and side of the house. The houses are pieced in many different colors, but the effect can be just as pleasing if only one or two colors are used. Whatever the choice, this quilt makes a delightful bedspread for a child's room.

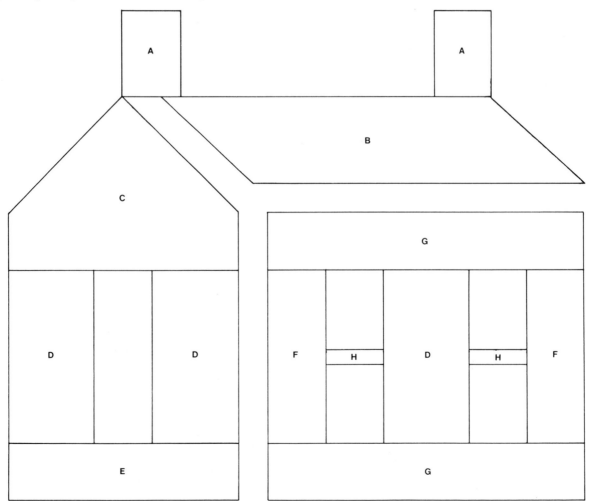

PIECING DIAGRAM.

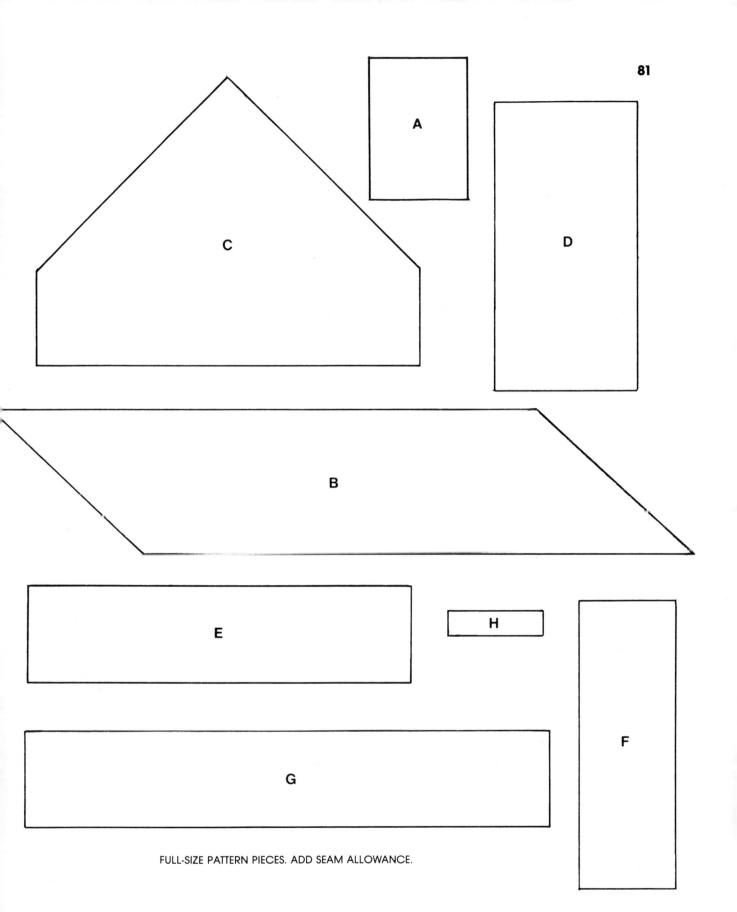

81

A

C

D

B

E

H

F

G

FULL-SIZE PATTERN PIECES. ADD SEAM ALLOWANCE.

19. Nine-Patch

Evolved from the basic one-patch form, the Nine-Patch and its many variations have been popular since the early 1800s. The design has been made in every imaginable size, color, and fabric. Wool and cotton examples abound, though rarer pieces in silk, satin, chintz, and velvet exist as well. The Nine-Patch was a favorite of the Amish and Mennonites and of more worldly quilters, too: most young women had at least one apiece in their hope chests.

Made in Lancaster County, Pennsylvania, at the turn of the century, the quilt illustrated on the opposite page may have been the first large piece made by a young Amish girl who was just establishing her proficiency as a seamstress. The pattern provides the classic first piece for the novice quilter today. Nine-Patch is easy to cut and piece, as all the seams run along straight lines. Dividing and subdividing the squares within the Nine-Patch can produce such other variations as Stars and Bear's Paw, but the example depicted here is the most straight-forward of Nine-Patch designs and is an excellent one for the beginner to attempt.

Nine large blocks form the central field. In each of five of the large blocks are nine smaller blocks; in each of five of these are nine tiny blocks. In bright orange and two shades of blue, this quilt exhibits the maker's wonderful facility with limited color. She must have used up the supply of small dark blue patches after completing the first, perfectly symmetrical patch (in the upper right hand corner), for the tiny blue patches are placed in random fashion in the three other large corner blocks. Or, perhaps she realized, after making the first patch, that the finished piece would not be half so interesting if each large nine-patch were uniform. In the center nine-patch, all of the small blocks are orange and light blue; this design choice adds coherence and grace to the composition and emphasizes the diagonal and crisscrossing motifs which run through the field. The uncomplicated quilting on the narrow and wide matching borders beautifully complements the simple design. Color is crucial in the Nine-Patch pattern, and the quilter should carefully plan the placement of each shade on a piece of graph paper before beginning to cut and piece.

Nine-Patch

SIZE: Approximately 52″ x 60″

One of the most straight-forward and easily pieced patterns, the Nine-Patch is perfect for the beginner. Before beginning, the maker should plot out the design on a piece of graph paper and make decisions about color and placement. Either the person who created the antique example shown here did not plan carefully, or she liked the look of the randomly placed small squares, for the elements in this quilt are far from symmetrical. (Compare the overall photograph and the piecing diagram.)

Squares of three different sizes are required for this pattern. The small squares (B) are 1½″. The medium squares (A) are 4½″, and the largest squares (the plain patches that alternate with the graphic patches) are 13½″. To recreate the quilt, twenty-four "A" pieces, two hundred and ten "B" pieces, and four of the largest squares (13½″) are required.

This quilter used a fairly wide border—it is approximately 10″ on two sides and 6″ on the other two. A ¾″ binding finishes the composition.

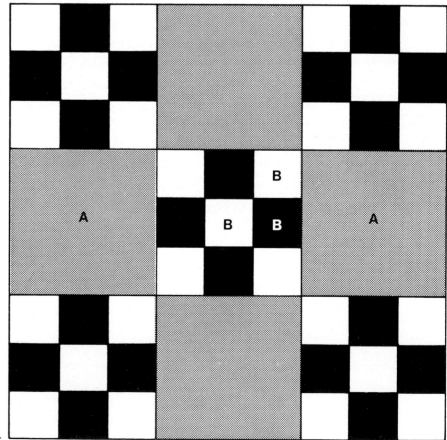

PIECING DIAGRAM.

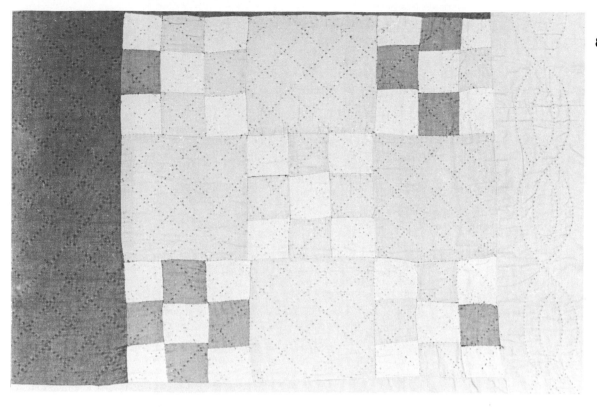

FULL-SIZE PATTERN PIECES.
ADD SEAM ALLOWANCE.

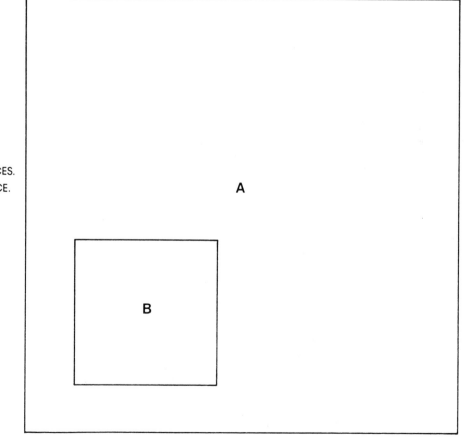

A

B

20. Grandmother's Flower Garden

An elegant Victorian piece, the stunning interpretation of Grandmother's Flower Garden illustrated on the opposite page was executed in Pennsylvania circa 1880. A variation of the one-patch, the pattern is composed of hexagons which can be arranged in any number of combinations to produce designs with such names as Mosaic, Honeycomb, and French Bouquet. This quiltmaker chose to emphasize the floral motif: six hexagonal petals of richly colored silk surround each cream-colored grosgrain center. Around each flower are twelve black silk hexagons which come together to form the somber field. The quilt is framed with a gold and black ribbon and a border of maroon shot with gold.

The small size (70″ square) and good condition of this piece indicate that it was probably used as a throw in the parlor, perhaps over the piano, or as a wrap suitable for a cool evening. Decorative quilts of this sort were produced during the Victorian period as much for show as for utility.

Relatively easy to piece, Grandmother's Flower Garden has long been a favorite among scrap-bag quilters. Interest revived in the pattern during the Depression years. The small size of the individual patches meant that almost every old scrap could be put to use, and the quilter never had to worry about matching flowers. In fact, the pattern is most effective when colors vary. Nevertheless, the best results come from careful overall color planning, as too much contrast can render the quilt rather garish and unseemly.

Grandmother's Flower Garden and its variations have been made in all areas of North America and in every size and material, though cotton's ubiquity and low price have made it the preferred material. Produced by the Amish and Mennonites as well as other quilters, early designs were usually executed in strong colors. Later examples often utilized the printed pastels in vogue during the early decades of this century.

Grandmother's Flower Garden

SIZE: Approximately 72" x 78"

This lovely pattern can be used to make a dramatic silk throw for the living room or a delightful cotton quilt for a guest room. Though not terribly difficult to piece, Grandmother's Flower Garden requires careful planning and accurate sewing so that each of the many tiny hexagons in the pattern will fit together. Before beginning to cut, a cardboard template should be made from the full-size pattern piece provided here. Remember to leave ¼" extra on each of the six sides when cutting.

The easiest way to piece the design is to sew each of the many flowers needed, and then to piece the hexagons of the background color (in this case, black) between them. This quilter has made thirteen rows of twelve complete flowers which are arranged in offset rows. Alternate rows have flowers on each end with only two-thirds of the flower showing. At the top and bottom of the quilt, one-half of a colored petal shows at the edge of the ribbon border.

Each of the floral motifs is pieced with seven hexagonal pieces. In this quilt the center of each flower is made of the same fabric; the petals are different plain and printed silks. In most flowers only one fabric is used for the petals; in a few, two fabrics alternate. If a striped fabric is used, it is essential that the stripes all point in the same direction.

A ⅝"-wide border made of embroidered ribbon frames the composition. The outer border is 2½" wide.

21. Sailboats

WHAT could be more appealing on a child's bed than a quilt covered with boats afloat on a calm sea? This charming quilt is made from a very unsophisticated pattern which requires minimal piecing and is relatively simple to assemble. A pattern of recent vintage, this delightful design seems to have emerged as late as the 1930s. Its popularity spread rapidly—even among the Mennonites and the Amish. Amish examples can be recognized by the somber background colors and the electric shades of the ships and borders. Mennonite quilters have characteristically chosen a white or off-white background and a strong color for the boats and borders. Since Sailboats is a pattern which is traditionally made for small children, these quilts tend to be pieced of easily washable cotton and made in small sizes—from crib to single bed—though larger examples can be found.

The boat and background are composed of sixteen small squares, some of which are patched in diagonal half-squares to form the illusion of bow, stern, sails, sea, and sky. Two full squares and two half squares are pieced together to form the trapezoid which is the hull of the boat; the sails are formed from four half-squares. Eight full and six half-squares are used to form the background for the boat. The light sailboats in the quilt opposite stand out exceptionally well against the darker ground. In a simple repetitive design such as this one, color choice is critical. Sometimes the ships are executed in a number of different colors, with one shade being repeated in the border.

Once the sailboats are pieced together the quilter must decide how to arrange them. In most cases the composition is similar to the one illustrated here, though the number of boats within the grid can vary; the rows can be arranged in series of four across and five down, five across and seven down, and so on. Occasionally, square examples of the Sailboats quilt are found, though the rectangular shape is standard.

Sailboats

SIZE: Approximately 63" x 78"

This charming pattern is easy to piece and when finished makes a wonderful bedspread for any child's room. Only four different pattern pieces are needed to make both the graphic patch and the grid, and as few as two colors are required. For those who prefer something more colorful, numerous bright shades can be substituted. The quilt illustrated here was worked in only two colors, and the effect is delightfully cool and airy.

If the modern maker wishes to recreate this quilt precisely, six white "A" pieces, four blue "A" pieces, one white and two blue "B" pieces, and one blue "C" piece are all that are required to make each of the graphic patches. The "C" pieces are 12" long and 3" wide.

The white grid between the boats is formed entirely from "C" and "D" pieces, the latter being 3" squares. The simple white border which surrounds the composition is the same width as the grid (3"), and the quilt is finished with a narrow binding of the same blue as the background color.

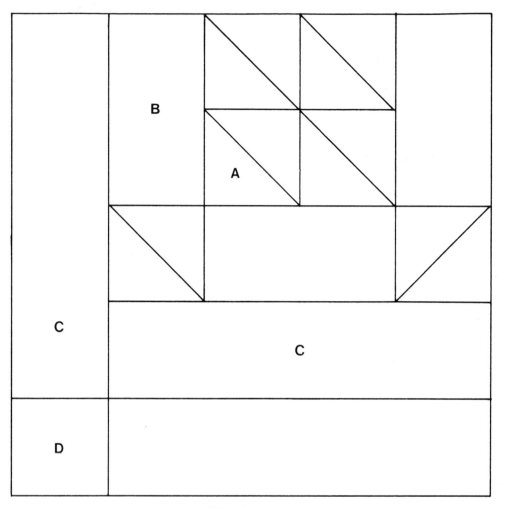

PIECING DIAGRAM.

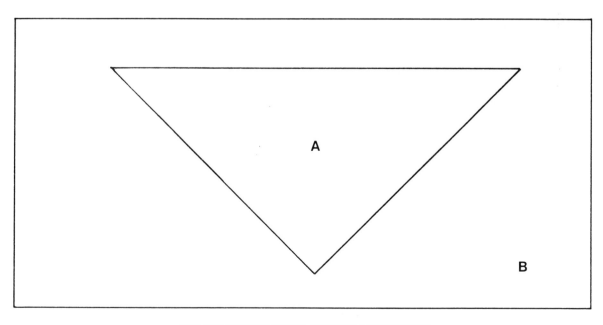

FULL-SIZE PATTERN PIECES. ADD SEAM ALLOWANCE.

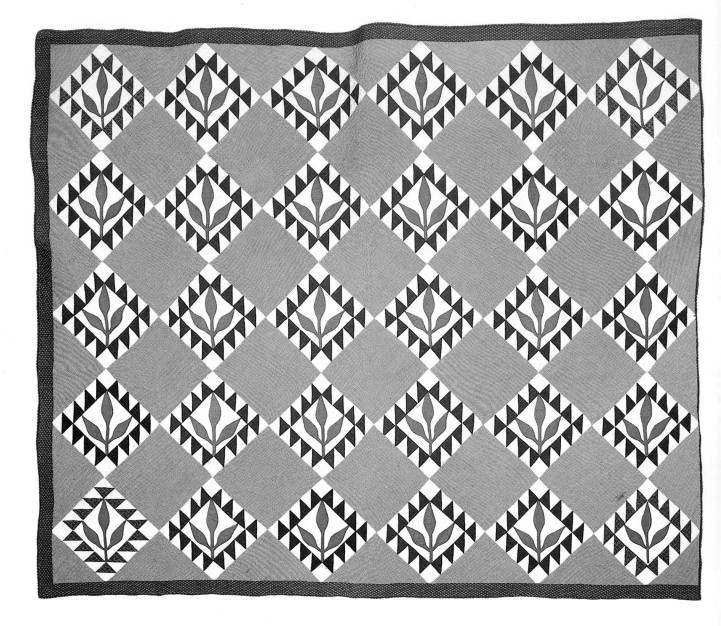

22. Peapod Leaf

On occasion a quilter will decide that he or she has had enough of copying classic patterns and that it is time to attempt a truly original, one-of-a-kind piece. Inspired both by nature and by motifs found on patterns previously made or seen, the adventurous quilter will devise a new block pattern. If the design is admired by other craftspeople, the new pattern may be copied extensively. This charming pattern is one such unique creation and probably comes from Pennsylvania. It is thought to date from 1880.

The graphic blocks are quite simple, with alternating brown and white half-squares pieced around a white central square. Once finished, the large pieced squares are set on the diagonal and arranged in rows of six across and five down, alternating with plain blocks of soft pink cotton. Inside each of the pieced frames created by the brown and white half-squares, the quilter has appliquéd three graceful leaves on a stem. Any number of variations of this pattern could be easily produced by simply changing the motif appliquéd within the squares, by changing the orientation of the patches, or by adding a larger pieced or appliquéd border.

Most quilters find that the freedom to choose colors, fabrics, placement of theme pieces, types of borders, and styles of quilting is quite sufficient to satisfy their creative needs. Peapod Leaf is an admirable example to follow. However, new quilt designs can only arise out of the imagination and artistic experimentation of individuals, and the time-tested patterns would not exist today were it not for the quilters who, in centuries past, tried something original. Peapod Leaf is merely a descriptive name for a one-of-a-kind quilt; it might just as well be appliquéd with a tulip or lily. So experimentation is recommended—but only at your own risk!

Peapod Leaf

Size: Approximately 75″ x
87″

This charming and unusual
pattern is excellent for the
beginner as it allows the maker
to practice both appliqué and
piecing techniques. The frame
(formed from the half-squares

"A" and squares "B") which
surrounds the central motif in
each graphic patch is easily
pieced in two contrasting colors—in this case, brown and
white were used.

PIECING DIAGRAM.

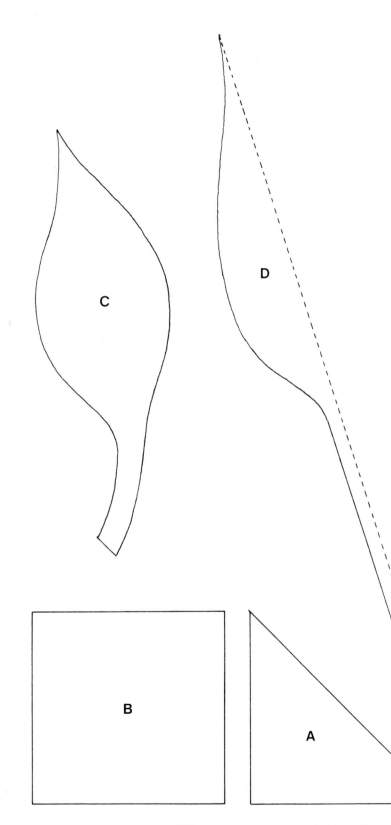

The pattern pieces (D and C) which make up the leaves and the stem are provided here, but the modern quilter may wish to appliqué an original design or several different motifs in the graphic patches.

The pattern piece "D" should be traced and then cut out of a piece of folded paper to make the full-size pattern piece. The pattern piece "C" is used to make both side leaves. When cutting out the leaf to be placed on the left side of the stem, the pattern piece must be reversed. Don't forget to leave enough room for making seams.

Note that the quilter who made this piece changed the orientation of the half-squares in the frame in the one graphic patch in the lower lefthand corner. This may be the "intentional" error found in many old quilts. It is an optional feature for the modern quilter.

FULL-SIZE PATTERN PIECES. ADD SEAM ALLOWANCE.

23. Fox and Geese

A CHARMING variation of the Hourglass pattern, Fox and Geese is an uncomplicated design which makes a vivid and pleasing composition. Though this pattern has been a favorite since the 18th century, few antique examples have survived and those that have are, for the most part, worn and faded. Fox and Geese was put to everyday use, not treasured as a showpiece.

The pattern is easy to piece, fabrics from the scrap bag are perfect for this design, and the finished product adds a brilliant accent to any room. The example illustrated was made by a Mrs. Giegle in Cumberland County, Pennsylvania, around 1880. She had a wonderful sense of color: the plain squares of vibrant scarlet calico contrast beautifully with the plain white and pale pink, tan, and blue calicoes in the graphic patches. Other color combinations can be equally as effective and the composition can be changed in numerous ways. For instance, rather than placing the squares on an axis so that they appear to be diamond-shaped (as in the quilt illustrated here), they can be turned forty-five degrees and arranged as squares. The quilter may choose to alternate graphic patches with solid patches or to eliminate solid patches entirely. The arrangement of hourglasses and colors may vary from patch to patch as it does in the illustrated quilt. Early quilters almost always made intentional "mistakes" so as not to offend God by making their work too perfect.

Variations of this pattern are numerous; many of the names are used interchangeably with Fox and Geese. The differences in the patterns may be as simple as a change in the orientation of the squares and half-squares which make up the individual patches. Among the other types are Old Maid's Puzzle, Double X, Flocks of Birds, Ladies' Wreath, Crosses and Losses, and Birds in the Air. The permutations seem infinite, and the quilter may want to arrange these shapes in an original design.

This quilt has been enormously popular in all areas of the country. It has been made for beds of every size including crib, trundle, single, double, and four-poster. Cotton examples are prevalent, but pieces done in wool and in silk can be found. A few fine examples using chintzes have survived from the early 1800s.

Fox and Geese

SɪᴢE: Approximately 64″ x 75″

This very traditional design is easy to piece and can be made by beginning quilters. The example illustrated here is double-bed size and is made up of thirty graphic patches which are set on the diagonal. These and the plain patches are arranged in offset rows. Each patch is 8″ square.

The quilter should treat each of the graphic patches as a unit of four four-patches. Piecing can then be done methodically, one four-patch at a time. Note that by changing the orientation of the finished graphic patches, the appearance of the quilt block may be changed.

The color scheme must be carefully planned in advance. Rich, contrasting colors are essential to the success of this quilt.

FULL-SIZE PATTERN PIECES.

ADD SEAM ALLOWANCE.

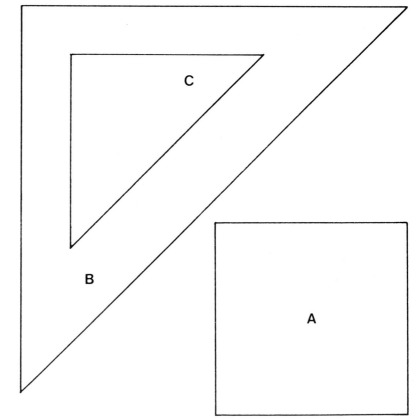

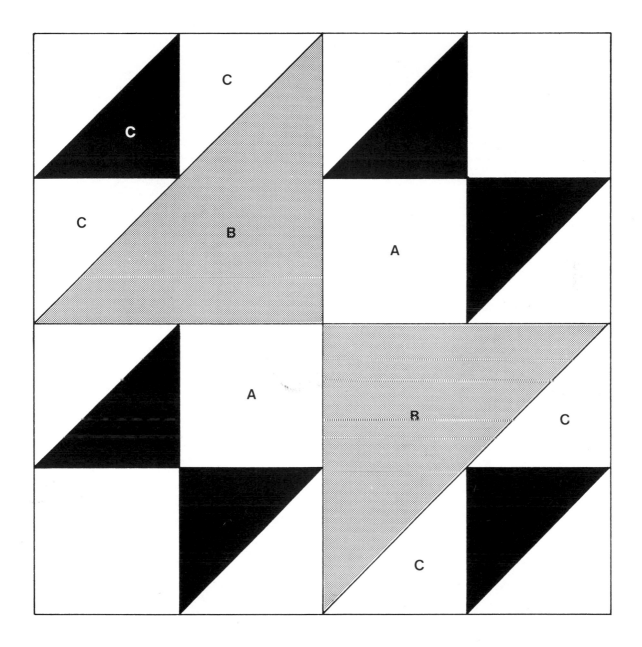

PIECING DIAGRAM.

24. Baskets

AN old and time-tested pattern, Baskets has been made in a multitude of styles. The one element that seems to remain constant throughout is the basket itself: its contents can vary from fruit to flowers to bits of triangular-shaped colored fabric, but the basket is almost always constructed in the same manner and bears close resemblance to an anvil. Often the basket is empty, and an appliquéd arched or pieced sawtooth handle is added to the top or sides. Commonly, as in the example illustrated on the opposite page, the illusion is of a basket heaped with mysterious contents, their identification left to the imagination of the viewer.

The creation of each basket is relatively simple and, in the basic form of this quilt, both the basket and contents are made up of half-squares of the same size. In the case of the illustration at hand, the basket is created in one solid color (in many examples, the half-squares used to make the basket are of alternating dark and light fabric). To form the contents of the basket, multi-colored half-squares are arranged in rows which ascend toward one corner of the square in which the basket is contained: as the triangles rise from the basket, the rows become smaller and take on a pyramidal shape. The half-squares at the ends of each row are done in the background color, in this case, white.

The arrangement of the baskets is of primary importance in the composition of this design. In the example opposite, the baskets are placed in horizontal offset rows. Sometimes baskets appear within grids, or a basket patch may alternate with an appliquéd flower patch. Quite often, baskets are arranged with their handles or contents facing the middle of the quilt; viewed from one side or the other, half the baskets appear to be upside down. Some Baskets quilts are made with ornate appliquéd borders of meandering flowers and vines; others have only a simple narrow binding in one of the quilt's dominant colors.

Popular since the middle of the last century, the Baskets pattern has been produced in wool, cotton, and silk, though solid cottons and cotton calicoes are prevalent. The most popular color combination has always been red and green against a white ground. Appropriate for both the child's and the adult's bedroom, this design has been made in every size from crib to the latter-day equivalent of king size.

Baskets

SIZE: Approximately 82" x 90½"

Though all the elements of the basket patches in this elegant quilt are sewn along straight lines, the great number of tiny pieces required to form each patch makes this design suitable only for an experienced quilter.

Four pattern pieces (A, B, C, D) are all that are required to form the elements of the entire quilt. For each patch, twenty-five "C" pieces, one "A" piece,

one "B" piece, and two "D" pieces are needed. The maker of the illustrated example chose an interesting way in which to finish her quilt: instead of creating a border around the graphic patches, she has used incomplete baskets which appear to float off the field.

Altogether, there are forty-five completed baskets and twenty-one incomplete ones. A narrow binding is the sole finishing touch.

PIECING DIAGRAM.

C

B

A

Instead of using a grid between the baskets, one device commonly used, this quilter has arranged the forms edge to edge in a pleasing manner. Each of the finished basket patches is 11¼″ square, and the completed quilt is large enough to cover a queen-sized bed.

Though Baskets quilts are most often made in red and white, rich saturated colors—as illustrated here—can be equally effective. There are numerous variations of the Baskets design, and these should be studied carefully for color schemes and patterns before the modern quilter undertakes such an extensive project.

D

FULL-SIZE PATTERN PIECES. ADD SEAM ALLOWANCE.

25. Sugar Loaf

In the 18th and early-19th centuries, sugar was often scarce and was therefore a commodity of great value. Sugar Loaf derives its name from this essential product, which, when available, could be bought in packages that were shaped like cones. Inside the blue protective paper, the sugar was firmly packed and rock hard; solid pieces were cut from the cone, placed in a mortar, and ground into powder with a pestle. Perhaps the quilter or quilters who first created this pattern had images of dozens of triangular sugar loaves arranged on kitchen shelves.

An unusual and exceptionally effective design, Sugar Loaf is simple to plan and piece. Each loaf is formed from ten small diamond pieces which are set in rows to form a pyramid. Five triangular pieces form the base. The completed loaves are placed in offset rows with inverted triangles of the background fabric between each loaf. This design is reminiscent of other patterns which are constructed from many small diamonds, such as Star of Bethlehem (Chapter 28) and Broken Star (Chapter 8). Though these well-known patterns are more difficult to piece, Sugar Loaf's singular design can be equally impressive if the quilter chooses colors carefully.

Made in the last quarter of the 19th century in Green County, Kentucky, by Mary Katherine Smith, the quilt illustrated opposite reflects the seamstress's exceptional color sense and thoughtful planning. Though she used dozens of different calicoes, prints, and solids to make up the 2,265 pieces used in this design, Mary Smith created a unity and coherence uncommon among quilts constructed from scraps. In each loaf, she arranged the diamond shapes in contrasting rows of light and dark; the five half-diamonds are of plain white cotton throughout, a design detail which serves to integrate this marvelous, beautifully-made composition.

Sugar Loaf

SIZE: Approximately 76″ x 80″

An unusual and visually exciting pattern, Sugar Loaf is relatively easy to piece if the maker is patient enough to cut and sew the 2,265 pieces necessary to complete the design. It is suggested that cardboard templates be made from the pattern pieces (A, B, C) provided here, so that, in cutting the fabric, all of the diamonds and triangles will be standard. Leave ¼″ extra on all sides for the seams.

This quilt consists of thirteen rows of sugar loaves with thirteen-and-a-half loaves in each row. Each of the 169 whole triangles is pieced in the same manner. Light rows alternate with dark rows of diamonds (B), and white triangles are pieced along the base (C). (Note the half-triangles which appear on one end of each row of sugar loaves). Between each of the graphic triangles is placed an inverted plain triangle (A) of the background fabric.

The border is 2″ wide; the fabric used is the same as that used for the plain triangles. The careful observer will see that the border is sewn onto only three sides of the quilt. A ⅜″ binding finishes the composition.

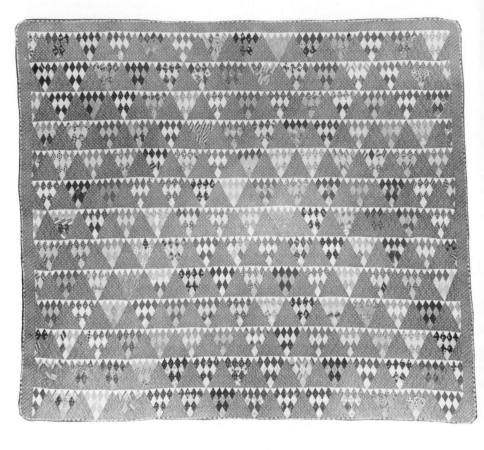

FULL-SIZE PIECING DIAGRAM.

FULL-SIZE PATTERN PIECES. ADD SEAM ALLOWANCE.

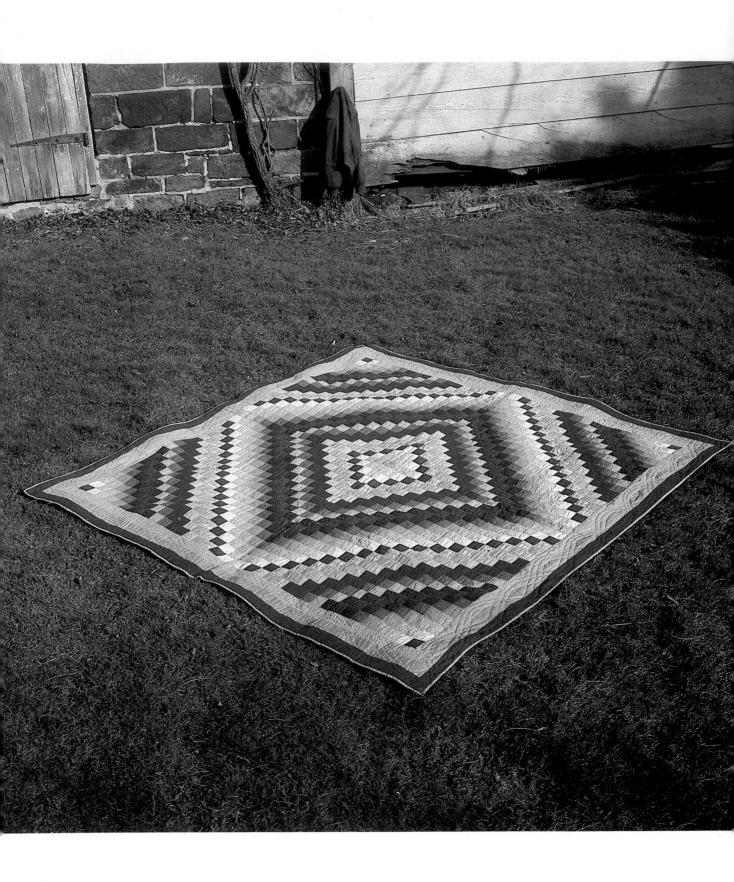

26. Sunshine and Shadow

THE lyrical name of this vibrant pattern seems an almost poetic translation of its abstract and geometric design. Named for the rows of squares which are arranged to lead the viewer's eye in and out among bands of brilliant color and sunshine and into more subdued areas of shadow, this is one of the most popular patterns among the Amish and the Mennonites, and one which seems to reflect their deep concern with nature as well as their ability to make the most abstract pattern expressive.

First made in the Amish areas of Illinois, Indiana, Iowa, Missouri, Ohio, and Eastern Pennsylvania in the late 1800s, the earliest and most prized examples of this pattern were executed in fine wools. Later, cotton and silk were widely employed. Mennonite quilts, like the sect's way of life, are slightly less austere in the shadowy areas than those made by the Amish. The Mennonite quilter who made the example illustrated here used many calico pieces in her work. Calico is almost never seen in Amish quilts; printed fabric is used only for backing, if at all. In general, Sunshine and Shadow quilts were made to fit beds from trundle to double size.

Though it is time consuming, the piecing of Sunshine and Shadow is not complicated. A total of 1,369 small square pieces is needed to make the central portion of this quilt. The number of patches of each color for each row must be carefully calculated before beginning. In this case, the small square pieces are set on the diagonal and sewn together from the outer corner toward the center until a complete square is formed. Three more corresponding squares and an extra vertical and horizontal row in the center are pieced and then placed together to form the diamond shape. The width of the bands of "sunshine" and "shadow" are placed irregularly and reflect individuality and personal flair in each composition. In many Amish examples, the pieced squares are not placed to form concentric diamonds; rather, they are pieced in square or rectangular form and may be set in simple vertical and horizontal rows rather than on the diagonal.

There are numerous variations on this simple one-patch pattern. Trip Around the World (see Chapter 15) and Grandma's Dream are names that are often used interchangeably with Sunshine and Shadow. Trip Around the World, however, does not always reflect the color choices which give Sunshine and Shadow its name. Checkerboard, another variation, is made by using two alternating colors to form a checkerboard pattern. Blocks, a perfect design for the scrap bag quilter, is made by arranging squares of varying colors in any number of ways.

Sunshine and Shadow

SIZE: Approximately 79″ square

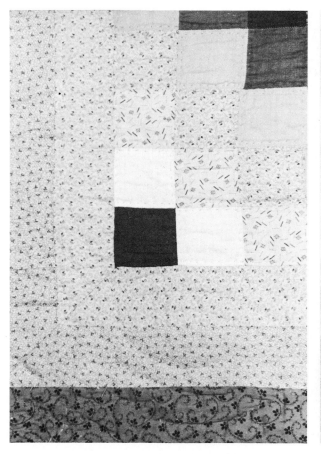

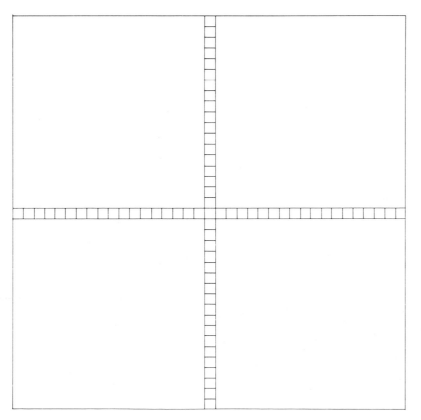

PIECING DIAGRAM.

A bright and effective pattern, Sunshine and Shadow is an ideal choice for the beginning quilter. A version of the one-patch, this quilt is pieced entirely from 2″ squares. Though the actual sewing is not difficult, Sunshine and Shadow must be carefully planned first as it is necessary to have enough fabric to complete each of the concentric squares and because color choice and placement are crucial. It is suggested that the quilter plot out the design on graph paper prior to purchasing fabrics and certainly before beginning to cut.

Piecing of this quilt begins in one corner. The piecing diagram illustrated here corresponds with the lower righthand corner of the quilt. The patches are sewn in diagonal rows, and each patch in a single row is of the same fabric. Four squares consisting of eighteen horizontal rows are sewn together. Once these are finished a nineteenth row is added so that the pieces meet in the center. All in all, 1,369 2″ squares are required.

This quilter made an attractive design choice by finishing the piece with three borders, all about 1¾″ wide. Wider quilted borders have often been used by the Amish, but, however the borders are executed, this classic pattern is bound to impress.

PIECING DIAGRAM FOR THE NINETEENTH ROW.

27. Barn Raising/Log Cabin

MANY quilt names and themes reflect aspects of everyday life in rural areas. In 19th-century America, the raising of a new barn was a community event, and everyone came to take part in both the work and the merrymaking that followed once the building was completed. The light and dark concentric diamonds seen in the quilt illustrated on the opposite page are said to represent the lumber laid out on the ground before the raising of the structure began.

The arrangement of the colored logs in each block of Barn Raising is crucial to the success of the piece. Working in Monmouth County, New Jersey, around 1870, this quiltmaker chose to piece thirty-six silk blocks, largely in plain bands accented by an occasional plaid or print. White and pastel shades of blue, pink, green, and yellow contrast with saturated tones of orange, rust, maroon, deep blue, crimson, purple, black, and brown. The logs are arranged around black central squares.

Relatively complicated to piece because of the need for four different patch types (see photographs and diagrams on the following two pages), Barn Raising should not be attempted by inexperienced quilters. (Piecing techniques for Log Cabin-type quilts are detailed in Appendix A). Because the logs are sewn by turning them one on top of the other, none of the stitching ever shows. Little or no skill in working quilting designs, however, is needed as Log Cabin examples are rarely quilted. A thin plain border, as illustrated here, is also typical.

Variations on the Barn Raising pattern are numerous: Light and Dark, Streaks of Lightning, Straight Furrow, and Courthouse Steps are just a few. A change of design can be effected by simply altering the orientation of the blocks. While difficult to master, the pattern is one which many quilters have sought to imitate. Antique examples abound, and their study will aid immeasurably in achieving successful results.

Barn Raising/Log Cabin

SIZE: Approximately 64″ square.

PIECING DIAGRAMS.

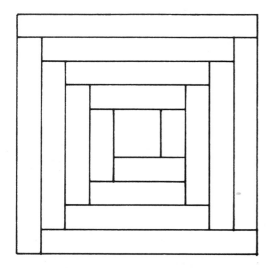

2	1	2	4	3	4
1	2	1	3	4	3
2	1	2	4	3	4
4	3	4	2	1	2
3	4	3	1	2	1
4	3	4	2	1	2

PIECING DIAGRAM.

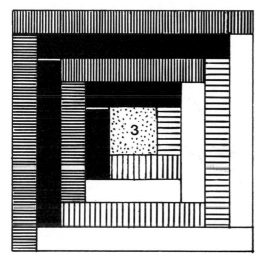

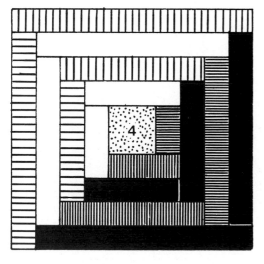

PIECING DIAGRAMS.

Difficult to piece because of the four different block types necessary, Barn Raising should be thought out carefully before beginning to sew, especially if the modern quilter wishes to re-create this quilt in such fine fabric as silk.

Carefully compare the four block types. (Blocks 1 and 2 appear in Chapter 1, p. 13). Four color tones are used: dark, medium-dark, light, and medium-light. The blocks differ only in the way the strips or logs are arranged. Note that in block 1 the two longest and outermost logs are pieced in the darkest fabric; in block 2 the lightest logs take this position. In block 3 these outermost logs are medium-dark, and in block 4 they are medium-light. From the center out, the placement of the blocks will differ slightly.

To make this quilt, eight "1" blocks, eight "3" blocks, ten "2" blocks, and ten "4" blocks are required. When finished, they are sewn together—as indicated in the piecing diagrams—to form a six-block by six-block square.

Every block in this quilt is 10″ square. The central 2″ square is surrounded by logs 1″ across and of varying lengths. When cutting the logs, be sure to leave ¼″ on the long sides and extra length on the ends which can be trimmed to the appropriate size. More detailed instructions on the backing and actual piecing of each block appear in Appendix A.

To finish the quilt, a simple border and/or binding should be added. In this case the bright red silk border is 2″ wide.

117

28. Star of Bethlehem

THIS vibrant crib quilt, with a brilliant central star and original appliquéd vine border, was acquired by the present owner with a note pinned to it which read, "Grandmother Fischer had this made for her daughter in 1864 or '65, outside Pittsburgh." Perhaps Mrs. Fischer's grandchild was expected during the holiday season, for star quilts of this sort were generally used on the bed only at Christmas time. The star was meant to represent the Star of Bethlehem, and the quilts were made in commemoration of the birth of Christ. Designs of this type, with rays emanating from a central eight-pointed star, are known variously as Star of Bethlehem, Star of the East, Lone Star, and Blazing Star. As these quilts were made for such a special and important season and were carefully packed away during the other months of the year, many fine examples dating from the last two hundred years have survived in excellent condition.

The Star of Bethlehem quilt is pieced point by point: forty-eight diamonds of equal size are arranged in rows of different lengths to form the eight diamond-shaped points. The middle and widest row is eight pieces across. When the points or rays are completed, they are attached to form the star.

Although cottons have been most commonly used because of their availability and low price, heavier fabrics such as chintz, wool, silk, satin, and velvet may have been favored whenever possible since these quilts were used at the coldest time of the year. Over time, quilters throughout North America have pieced this design in every conceivable color combination and size. Pastels can be just as effective as more electric shades; the vibrancy of the quilt depends upon the arrangement of harmonizing and contrasting colors in each of the star's points.

Variations on the eight-pointed star pattern are legion. The simplest is the LeMoyne Star (called Lemon Star in New England) which is made from eight diamond-shaped patches. Sunburst (also called Starburst) is a dramatic version of the star theme in which the diamond patches are never reduced in number to form points, but fill the entire field of the quilt. Often the borders which surround Star of Bethlehem quilts are the areas in which one sees most clearly the imaginative and original designs of an individual maker. Appliquéd flowers, birds, and small stars may surround the composition. Whether this brilliant star lies against a solid background with a plain binding or is surrounded with an ornate design or border, the quilt is a wonderful pattern for the modern quilter to recreate.

Star of Bethlehem

SIZE: Approximately 42″
square

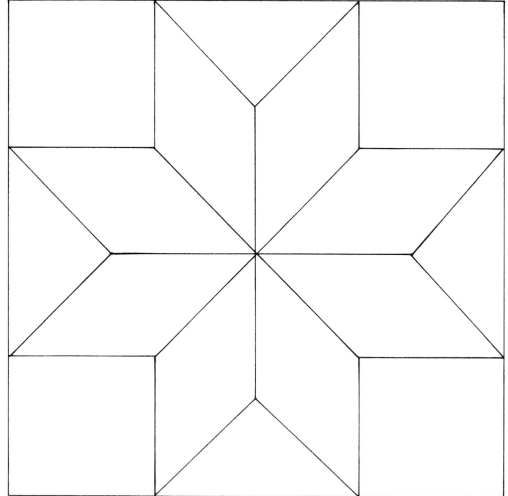

This beautiful crib quilt with its meandering vine border is appropriate for experienced quilters to recreate. The central Star of Bethlehem is eight-pointed; each of the points or rays are constructed from sixty-four tiny diamonds. These tiny pieces must be cut and pieced with special care or the star will not lie flat. Even a slight mistake in one of the eight points will keep them from fitting together. Before beginning to cut, make a template from the pattern piece provided here. When cutting the diamonds, be sure to add ¼″ on all sides for seam allowance. Pieced in fifteen rows, each ray is eight diamonds wide at the widest point.

The color key provides a list of the colors of the calicoes used by this maker, but the modern quilter may choose any color combination as long as each point is pieced in exactly the same way.

After the points have been completed and sewn together, 10″ squares are pieced in the corners between the points. Half-squares (made by cutting the 10″ squares on the diagonal) are pieced between the remaining points. A border and binding are then added to frame the finished star.

Since designs for appliquéd borders of this type are usually the original creations of the makers, patterns for the flowers and leaves are not supplied here. Quilters experienced with appliqué may wish to create their own designs. The border is 3¾″ wide; the binding is ⅝″.

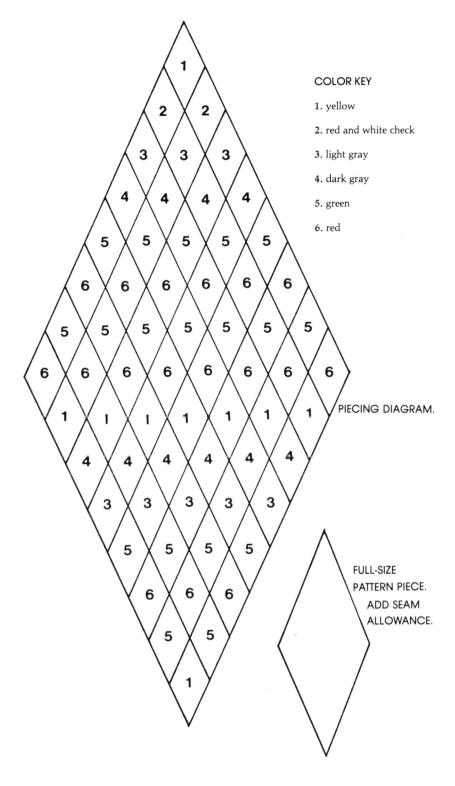

COLOR KEY

1. yellow

2. red and white check

3. light gray

4. dark gray

5. green

6. red

PIECING DIAGRAM.

FULL-SIZE
PATTERN PIECE.
ADD SEAM
ALLOWANCE.

29. Amish Bars

A STRIKINGLY simple geometric pattern, Bars has always been popular among the Amish and Mennonite people. One of the earliest American pieced quilt forms, this abstract pattern has traditionally been executed in rich, deep colors which seem as appropriate on the wall of a contemporary home as in the farmhouses of the "plain" people. This simple pattern is perfect for the beginning quilter to recreate: it requires a modicum of planning and color sense and allows large areas for the practice of quilting techniques.

Many of the finest of Bar quilts were made in Lancaster County, Pennsylvania. Wool was most commonly used in the 1800s and early 1900s; most cotton examples probably date from the 1920s and '30s. Rare silk and linen Bars can be found, though wool is the fabric most sought by collectors. The woolen trundle-bed quilt illustrated on the opposite page is somewhat faded with age and wear (children's blankets always get more use than those that rest in state on adults' beds) but it remains exemplary of the color sense of the Amish—bright, saturated colors contrast with a drab background.

Piecing this quilt is extremely simple. Seven bars of two alternating colors (in this case four of scarlet and three of Kelly green) make up the central area. The border is composed of simple, slightly narrower strips of light brown; a Kelly green binding finishes the composition with an elegant touch. So simple is the Bars pattern that many early quilters used it as the backing for quilts of more complicated design, rendering the finished quilt reversible. Lucky is the collector today who finds such an example.

There are numerous variations on the Bars form, all slightly more complex than this one, but equally popular among the Amish and the Mennonites. In a pattern known as Stripes, the bars cover the entire field, leaving no room for a border. Rainbow is much the same in composition, but the effect is produced by gradations of color rather than color contrast. Other variations include Joseph's Coat of Many Colors and Tree Everlasting.

Amish Bars

SIZE: 41" x 60"

This striking trundle-bed quilt
is simple to re-create. The
seven bars are 5" wide and 52"
long and are combined with a
3½"-wide border and a
½"-wide binding. Seam
allowances must be added
when cutting out the strips of
fabric.

Since piecing diagrams and pattern pieces are unnecessary for
such a simply constructed
quilt, several variations of the
Bars form are illustrated on
these pages. Quilt A is an example of Joseph's Coat of
Many Colors, one of the most
elaborate of Bars patterns. The
slanted border which repeats
the colors used in the center is
an interesting design variation.
This quilt was made in Pennsylvania circa 1900.

A

Quilt B is an interesting alternative to the plain Bars design. Instead of using just one bright saturated color in four of the central bars, squares in a variety of colors are pieced into strips. Intense and effective, this quilt was made by a member of a Pennsylvania Amish community around 1900.

A very unusual design, Quilt C is known as Sawtooth Bars and was made in Pennsylvania around 1870. Slightly more difficult to make than the other examples, it requires the piecing of strips of contrasting half-squares along each side of the bars and around the border.

Quilt D is a choice example of the Amish Bars design. Note the narrow frame around the central bars, the wide border, and the corner squares. The quilt was made in Lancaster County, Pennsylvania, around 1895.

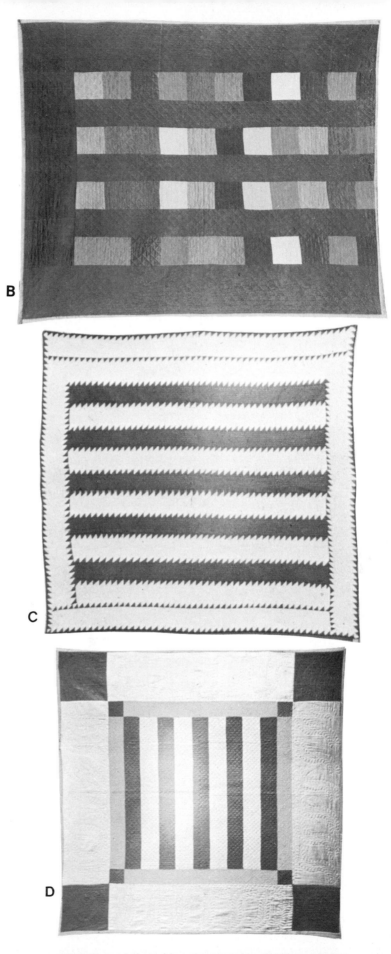

30. Hawaiian-Style

ALMOST every child has made valentines or snowflakes by folding a piece of construction paper in half, quarters, or eighths, and then cutting out a design. When the paper is unfolded, intricate but symmetrical patterns emerge. If the paper is colored and placed against a plain white background or pasted to a doily, the cut-out is shown to best effect. Pennsylvania-German quilters recognized the possibilities of this childhood pastime for their craft, and they produced many interesting appliquéd quilts using the method they called *scherenschnitte* (scissor cuttings). Though the Pennsylvania-Germans used this appliqué technique long before the women of Hawaii, quilts of this style have come to be thought of as Hawaiian, as the quilters in those tropical islands produced *only* pieces of this type.

Quilting was brought to Hawaii in the 19th century by the wives of missionaries. Hawaiian royalty and their attendants were taught to use needle and thread, and were probably shown some pieced quilt designs. The Hawaiians, however, preferred this method of appliqué, as it allowed them to produce original and abstract patterns reflecting the exotic flowers, plants, and trees of their native land. Their bold and beautiful pieces are highly valued and much sought after today.

In general, appliquéd Hawaiian-style quilts produced on the mainland are more representational than their island counterparts. Hearts, birds, tulips, leaves, snowflakes, and other distinctly recognizable objects are often part of mainland designs. The quilts illustrated opposite were both made on the Eastern seaboard: the larger in New England around 1890, the smaller in Eastern Pennsylvania approximately twenty years earlier.

In most examples of this appliqué style, the design is cut from one color and set against a white or off-white background. The Hawaiians at first limited themselves to red on white, but later color schemes were more varied—strong shades of yellow, red, orange, green, or pink were used against a white ground. Occasionally, examples with a colored ground are found, though printed or multi-colored fabrics are never used in a true Hawaiian quilt, and are rare in those produced on the mainland. Both mainland and island examples usually consist of one large pattern cut from a single piece of fabric, but smaller designs can be cut and arranged on the ground, as in the large quilt shown here. The addition of a border design is optional.

Hawaiian-Style

SIZE: Approximately 30″ x 30″

Hawaiian-style quilts are usually made from one symmetrical design which is cut out of a single piece of fabric and appliquéd to a plain piece of material. Sometimes, as in one of the examples illustrated, there are numerous designs appliquéd to the field. In other quilts, there is one design enclosed within a border. The patterns for the central motif of the crib quilt and its border are provided here.

Six pieces of fabric will be needed to make this quilt. The first, for the background, should be about one square yard. The piece from which the central motif can be cut should be 17″ x 17″, and the border must be made from four pieces 4″ wide. Two strips of these should be about 26″ long; the other two about 17″.

To make the motif, fold the 17″ x 17″ piece in half, then in fourths, and then into a triangle. The design given on the opposite page can be traced onto paper and then pinned to the fabric with the edge indicated placed on the bias. Follow the edge of the pattern, leaving at most ¼″ for seam allowance, cutting with extremely sharp scissors. When the piece is cut out and unfolded, its center should be placed in the exact center of the background piece. The symmetrical design is then pinned on and appliquéd to the field.

To make the border, mark off the 26″ strips of fabric into tenths and fold in an accordion-like manner. Pin the pattern piece to the fabric and cut out the pattern. The strips should unfold into five continuous border motifs. Repeat the same procedure with the shorter strips, only this time folding the fabric into sixths. This will yield three border motifs. These should be appliquéd around the central design (as shown in the black and white photograph).

When the designs have been appliquéd, turn back the edges of the background fabric, trim, and seam. Rather than following the original design exactly, allow the background material to extend 1½" beyond each of the four borders. This will show off the design to better effect. Then add a ½" binding in the same color as the central motif and the borders.

FULL-SIZE PATTERN PIECES. ADD SEAM ALLOWANCE.

Appendix A

FULL-SIZE PATTERN PIECES. ADD SEAM ALLOWANCE.

A multitude of designs can be made from Log Cabin blocks, but the individual blocks themselves are always sewn in the same manner. Usually a piece of white muslin slightly larger than the size of the finished block (7¼″ square for Streaks of Lightning, 10″ square for Barn Raising) is used as backing.

The central squares and logs for each block are cut out, allowing an extra ¼″ of fabric for the seams. To begin sewing the block, the small central square is sewn to the exact center of the muslin with the right side up. The extra ¼″ of fabric is not tucked under when sewing. Then the shortest log is added to the square. The log is placed right side down on top of the square and sewed ¼″ from the edge (over the first seam made on the central square). When the first seam is finished, the log is turned over so that it is right side up. The ends are trimmed to the proper length (allowing an extra ¼″) and the log is pressed into place. Then, proceeding clockwise, the next log is added and pressed. Continue to add logs of increasing length until the required number of strips has been pieced to each side and the outermost of the concentric squares is reached.

Be sure to study the diagrams for blocks 1, 2, 3, and 4, as placement of the different colored logs varies in the making of each one. Once the desired number of blocks has been reached, these blocks are pieced together to form the chosen pattern. Windmill Blades (Chapter 5) is pieced in much the same way, though

eight sides are made instead of just four. To make Courthouse Steps, another variation of the Log Cabin, the blocks are arranged somewhat differently. The blocks illustrated here can be used to make not only the patterns described in this book, but also such lovely variations as Dark and Light and Straight Furrow, details of which are illustrated here.

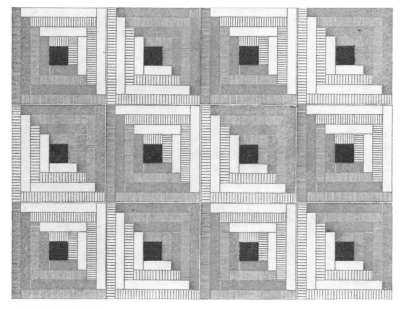

STRAIGHT FURROW.

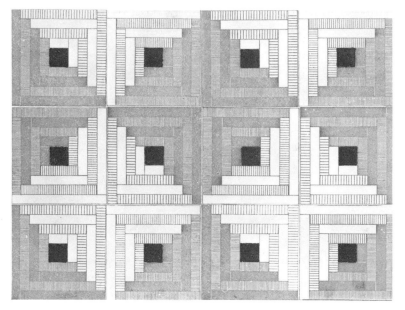

DARK AND LIGHT.

Quilt Supplies

PROPER materials for making traditional quilts can be found in some quality fabric shops and in the increasing number of specialized needlework and quilting outlets throughout North America. For those seeking hard-to-find fabrics and/or materials, the following suppliers are suggested. Those who will handle direct mail orders are indicated with an asterisk (*).

GENERAL
Fabrics, patterns, templates, instruction books, frames, and other supplies.

The Back Door
19 Broad Street
PO Box 1467
Sumter, SC 29150
(805) 775-5513

Bits + Pieces Quilt Shop
2 Enfield St.
Enfield, CT 06082
(203) 763-1530

* Come Quilt With Me
PO Box 1063
Brooklyn, NY 11202
(212) 377-3652

* Country Heirlooms
25 East Third Street
Hope, AR 71051
(501) 777-1566

Country Quilt Shop
58½ West Main St.
Westminster, MD 21157
(301) 848-2006

* Cross Patch
Route 9
Garrison, NY 10524
(914) 424-3443

The Freedom General Store
2 Church Street
Flemington, NJ 08822
(201) 788-3072

* Ginger Snap Station
PO Box 81086
Atlanta, GA 30366
(404) 455-4104

* Glad Creations, Inc.
3400 Bloomington Avenue S.
Minneapolis, MN 55407
(612) 724-1079

Granny's Trunk
4644 Cleveland Heights Blvd.
Country Corner Shopping Center
Lakeland, FL 33803
(813) 646-0074

* Gutcheon Patchworks
611 Broadway
New York, NY 10012
(212) 505-0305

Hearthside Quilts & Supplies
Church Hill Road
Charlotte, VT 05445
(802) 425-2198

* Orvilla's Quilts 'n Things
127 Washington Square
Washington, IL 61571
(309) 444-9212

* The Patch Basket
Box 38
Blooming Grove, NY 10914

Patchwork
25 North Gore Ave.
Webster Groves, MO 63119
(314) 961-2983

Quilt, Et Cetera
1500 South Highway 301
Dade City, FL 33525
(904) 567-7400

The Quilt Shop
4525 50th Street
Lubbock, TX 79414
(806) 793-2485

* Quilts and Other Comforts
6700 W. 44th Avenue, Box 394-0
Wheatridge, CO 50033
(303) 420-4272

Quilts and So Forth
8321 La Mesa Boulevard
La Mesa, CA 92041
(619) 464-1718

Quilter's Barn
46 South Main Street
Allentown, NJ 08501
(609) 259-2504

Quilt Square
13426 Clayton Road
St. Louis, MO 63131
(314) 878-4886

* Quiltwork Patches
43 NW Sixth Street
Box 724-Q6
Corvallis, OR 97339
(503) 754-1475

* The Silver Thimble Quilt Shop
249 High Street
Ipswich, MA 01938
(617) 356-7350

Zepora's Quilt Shop
Route 2 and Cressup Street
Belmont, WV 26134
(304) 665-2687

FABRICS PRIMARILY

Pierre Deux Fabrics
381 Bleecker St.
New York, NY 10014
(212) 675-4054

870 Madison Ave.
New York, NY 10021
(212) 570-9343

other branches in:
Boston, Seattle, San Francisco,
Beverly Hills, Bal Harbor,
Washington, DC, New Orleans,
Carmel, Houston, Dallas, Scotts-
dale, Kansas City, Chicago,
Atlanta, Palm Beach

* The Dorr Mill Store (wools)
Route 103
Guild, NH 03754
(603) 863-1197

* Heartfelt (wool batting)
Box 1829
Vineyard Haven, MA 02568

* Mary E. Bemus
Le Rouvray Antiquities (French
Cotton Prints)
Troy Corners Church
90 E. Square Lake Road
Troy, MI 48098
(313) 879-9848

Norton Candle and Handiwork
House (General)
1836 Country Store Village
Wilmington, VT 05363
(802) 464-5702

* Jane L. Perkins (General)
6 Waterville Street
North Grafton, MA 01536
(617) 839-3656

PATCHWORK SQUARES PRIMARILY

* Elizabeth's Patches
PO Box 2174
Waco, TX 76703

Patches, Inc.
1499 Washington Street
Route 3, Box 66
Harper's Ferry, WV 25425
(304) 535-6968

STENCILS, TEMPLATES, PATTERNS PRIMARILY

* The American Quilter
PO Box 7455
Menlo Park, CA 94025

* Bear's Paw Press
PO Box 3005
Fremont, CA 95438

* Featherbed Quilts
Gunstock Hill Road
RFD 7
Milford, NH 03246

* Patchwork Patterns
Box 3461
Industry, CA 91744
(213) 692-4135

* Victory Tool and Die Co., Inc.
131 Colvin Street
Rochester, NY 14611
(716) 235-6756

* The Whitacres
Box 153
Wellston, MI 49689
(616) 848-4218

STRETCHERS, FRAMES, RESTORATION

Pie Galinat (stretchers, restoration)
New York, NY
(212) 741-3259

* Heritage Woodcrafts, Inc. (frames)
2470 Dixie Highway
Pontiac, MI 48055
(313) 332-1494

* Magic Timber (frames)
143 Lawrence Ave.
Woodstock, IL 60098

Restorations (restoration)
382 11th Street
Brooklyn, NY 11215
(212) 788-7909

Antique Quilt Dealers

MANY of the dealers listed exhibit and sell their quilts largely at regional shows throughout the year. When not on the road, they often work out of their homes and meet with customers by appointment only.

ARIZONA

Antiques America
3000 East Broadway
Tucson, Arizona 85719
(602) 327-8693

Just Us on Court
299 North Court Avenue
Tucson, Arizona 85701
(602) 622-3607

CALIFORNIA

Kiracofe and Kile
955 Fourteenth Street
San Francisco, California 94114
(415) 431-1222

Peace and Plenty
1130 West Washington Boulevard
Venice, California 90291
(213) 396-8210

CONNECTICUT

Patty Gagarin Antiques
Banks North Road
Fairfield, Connecticut 06430
(203) 259-7332

DISTRICT OF COLUMBIA

Cherishables
1816 Jefferson Place, N.W.
Washington, D.C. 20036
(202) 785-4087

GEORGIA

Granny Taught Us How
1921 Peachtree Road, N.E.
Atlanta, Georgia 30309
(404) 351-2942

IDAHO

The Hissing Goose:
A Gallery of Fine Americana
Fourth and Leadville Streets
Box 597
Ketchum, Idaho 83340
(208) 726-3036

The Quilt Barn
Sonja Tarnay
Box 1252
421 South River and Elm
Hailey, Idaho 83333
(208) 788-4011

ILLINOIS

Carrow and McNerney
Country Antiques
Winnetka, Illinois 60693
(312) 441-7137 or 446-7516

Wild Goose Chase Quilt Gallery
526 Dempster
Evanston, Illinois 60202
(312) 328-1808

INDIANA

Alcorn's Antiques
Grace Alcorn
214 West Main Street
Centerville, Indiana 47330

Folkways
Susan Parett & Rod Lich
R. 2, Box 365
Georgetown, Indiana 47122
(812) 951-3454

KANSAS

Mark's International Oriental Rugs
   & Carpets
5512 Johnson Drive
Mission, Kansas 66202
(913) 722-2242

KENTUCKY

Folkworks
Shelley Zegart
Louisville, Kentucky
(502) 897-7566

Bruce and Charlotte Riddle
116 West Broadway
Bardstown, Kentucky 40004
(502) 348-2275

MARYLAND

"All of Us Americans" Folk Art
Bettie Mintz
Box 5943
Bethesda, Maryland 20014
(301) 652-8512

Stella Rubin
Query Mill Road
Gaithersburg, Maryland 20760
(301) 948-4187

Norma and William Wangel
American Antiques and Folk Art
Potomac, Maryland 20854
(302) 299-8430

MICHIGAN

American Horse
Sandra Mitchell
25009 Chambley
Southfield, Michigan 48034
(313) 352-5995

Plain Dealer
Jim and Klaudia Fisher
106 East High Street
Union City, Michigan 49094
(517) 741-3018

MINNESOTA

Attic Workshop Quilts
Bryce and Donna Hamilton
4033 Linden Hills Boulevard
Minneapolis, Minnesota 55410
(612) 920-6268

MISSOURI

Susan Davidson Antiques
4 Maryland Plaza
St. Louis, Missouri 63108
(314) 454-1020

Patchwork Sampler
Sharon Keith and Elizabeth Kramer
9735 Clayton Road
St. Louis, Missouri 63124
(314) 997-6116

NEW JERSEY

Tewksbury Antiques
The Crossroads
Oldwick, New Jersey 08858
(201) 439-2221

NEW YORK

America Hurrah Antiques
316 East 70th Street
New York, New York 10021
(212) 535-1930

American Antiques and Quilts
Thomas K. Woodard
835 Madison Avenue
New York, New York 10021
(212) 988-2906

American Country Antiques
Judith and James Milne
New York, New York
(212) 427-9642

American Folk Art Gallery
Steve Miller
17 East 96th Street
New York, New York 10028
(212) 348-5219

America's Folk Heritage Gallery
Jay Johnson
1044 Madison Avenue
New York, New York 10021
(212) 628-7280

Antique Buyers International, Inc.
790 Madison Avenue
New York, New York 10021
(212) 861-6700

Bonner's Barn
25 Washington Street
Malone, New York 12953
(518) 483-4001

Dalva Brothers, Inc.
44 East 57th Street
New York, New York 10022
(212) 758-2297

Edelmann Galleries, Inc.
123 East 77th Street
New York, New York 10021
(212) 628-1700

The Gazebo
660 Madison Avenue
New York, New York 10021
(212) 832-7077

Phyllis Haders Quilts:
Amish, Pieced, Appliqué
New York, New York
(212) 832-8181

Janos and Ross
110 East End Avenue
New York, New York 10028
(212) 988-0407

Ricco Johnson Gallery
475 Broome Street
New York, New York 10013
(212) 966-0541

Kelter-Malcé
361 Bleecker Street
New York, New York 10014
(212) 989-6760

Made in America
Wendy Lavitt
1234 Madison Avenue
New York, New York 10028
(212) 289-1113

Original Print Collectors Group,
   Ltd.
Corporate Art Division
215 Lexington Avenue
New York, New York 10016

Pillow Finery
979 Third Avenue, 709M
New York, New York 10022
(212) 935-7295

The Quilt Gallery
Main Street
Bridgehampton, New York 11932
(516) 537-9898

George E. Schoelkopf
1065 Madison Avenue
New York, New York 10028
(212) 879-3672

Judith Selkowitz Fine Arts, Inc.
25 West 56th Street
New York, New York 10022
(212) 586-2602

NORTH CAROLINA

Boone's Antiques, Inc.
Highway 301 South
Box 3796
Wilson, North Carolina 27893
(919) 237-1508

OHIO

Bruce and Margie Clawson
Blue Creek, Ohio 45616
(513) 544-3263

Drummer Boy Antiques
32 South High Street
Dublin, Ohio 43017
(614) 764-9380

Federation Antiques, Inc.
2030 Madison Road
Cincinnati, Ohio 45208
(513) 321-2671

Quilts and Country
Darwin D. Bearley
19 Grand Avenue
Akron, Ohio 44308
(216) 376-4965

Joan Townsend
4215 Utica Road
Lebanon, Ohio 45036
(513) 932-3619

PENNSYLVANIA

M. Finkel and Daughter
936 Pine Street
Philadelphia, Pennsylvania 19107
(215) 627-7797

James and Nancy Glazer Antiques
2209 Delancey Street
Philadelphia, Pennsylvania 19103
(215) 732-8788

Byron R. Kelley and Kenneth
 Raybuck
American Antiques
3336 Durham Road
Mechanicsville, Pennsylvania 18934
(215) 794-5013

The Pink House
On Route 179
in New Hope, Pennsylvania 18938
(215) 862-5947

J.D. Query Antiques
R.D. 2
Martinsburg, Pennsylvania 16662
(814) 793-3185

TENNESSEE

Bob and Donna Parrott
American Country Furniture and
 Accessories
433 Scenic Drive
Knoxville, Tennessee 37919
(615) 525-6359

TEXAS

Larry A. Mulkey & Associates
World Trade Center 9074
Box 58547
Dallas, Texas 75258
(214) 748-1361

Quilt Collections

MANY of the museums in the following list have extensive quilt collections; others have just a few fine examples. Because of the delicate nature of old textiles, most museums do not keep their quilts on view at all times. We suggest that those who wish to see the quilts in these museums and historical societies write or call to find out if the quilts are on exhibit or if they can be seen by special arrangement.

ALASKA

Anchorage Historical and Fine Arts
 Museum
121 West Seventh Avenue
Anchorage, Alaska 99501
(907) 279-1553

ARIZONA

Arizona Heritage Center
949 East Second Street
Tucson, Arizona 85719
(602) 628-5774

Fort Verde State Historical Park
Box 397, off Interstate 17
Camp Verde, Arizona 86322
(602) 567-3275

Pioneer Arizona
Box 11242
Interstate 17 and Pioneer Road
Phoenix, Arizona 85029
(602) 993-0210

CALIFORNIA

The Fine Arts Museum of San
 Francisco
M.H. de Young Memorial Museum
Golden Gate Park
San Francisco, California 94118
(415) 751-4432

Haggin Museum
1201 North Pershing Avenue
Stockton, California 95203
(209) 462-4116

COLORADO

Boulder Historical Society Museum
Broadway at Arapahoe
Boulder, Colorado 80302
(303) 449-3464

The Denver Art Museum
100 West 14th Avenue Parkway
Denver, Colorado 80204
(303) 575-2793

Greeley Municipal Museum
919 Seventh Street
Civic Center Complex
Greeley, Colorado 80631
(303) 353-6123, ext. 391

CONNECTICUT

The Mattatuck Museum
119 West Main Street
Waterbury, Connecticut 06702
(203) 753-0381

Stamford Historical Society, Inc.
713 Bedford Street
Stamford, Connecticut 06901
(203) 323-1975

Wadsworth Atheneum
600 Main Street
Hartford, Connecticut 06103
(203) 278-2670

Wilton Heritage Museum
249 Danbury Road
Wilton, Connecticut 06897
(203) 762-7257

DELAWARE

The Hagley Museum
Box 3630
Greenville, Wilmington, Delaware
   19807
(302) 658-2400

The Henry Francis du Pont Winterthur Museum
Winterthur, Delaware 19735
(302) 656-8591

DISTRICT OF COLUMBIA

Daughters of the American Revolu-
   tion
1776 D Street, N.W.
Washington, D.C. 20006
(202) 628-1776

National Museum of American
   History
(Smithsonian Institution)
Fourteenth Street and Constitution
   Avenue, N.W.
Washington, D.C. 20560
(202) 357-1300

FLORIDA

Florida State Museum
University of Florida
Gainesville, Florida 32611
(904) 392-1721

HAWAII

Bernice Pauahi Bishop Museum
1355 Kalihi Street
Honolulu, Hawaii 96819
(808) 847-3511

Honolulu Academy of Arts
900 South Beretania Street
Honolulu, Hawaii 96814
(808) 538-3693

ILLINOIS

Illinois State Museum
Corner Spring and Edwards Streets
Springfield, Illinois 62706
(217) 782-7386

KANSAS

Spencer Museum of Art
University of Kansas
Lawrence, Kansas 66045
(913) 864-4710

LOUISIANA

Louisiana State Museum
751 Chartres Street
New Orleans, Louisiana 70116
(504) 568-6968

MAINE

Camden-Rockport Historical
   Society
Camden, Maine 04843
(no phone)

York Institute Museum
375 Main Street
Saco, Maine 04072
(207) 282-3031

MARYLAND

Baltimore Museum of Art
Art Museum Drive
Baltimore, Maryland 21218
(301) 396-7101

Maryland Historical Society
201 West Monument Street
Baltimore, Maryland 21201
(301) 685-3750

Star-Spangled Banner Flag House
844 East Pratt Street
Baltimore, Maryland 21202
(301) 837-1793

MASSACHUSETTS

Essex Institute
132 Essex Street
Salem, Massachusetts 01970
(617) 744-3390

Fall River Historical Society
451 Rock Street
Fall River, Massachusetts 02720
(617) 679-1071

Fitchburg Historical Society
50 Grove Street
Fitchburg, Massachusetts 01420
(617) 345-1157

Historic Deerfield, Inc.
The Street
Deerfield, Massachusetts 01342
(413) 774-5581

Museum of Fine Arts
Huntington Avenue
Boston, Massachusetts 02115
(617) 267-9300

Old Sturbridge Village
Sturbridge, Massachusetts 01566
(617) 347-3362

Plymouth Antiquarian Society
Spooner House, 27 North Street
Plymouth, Massachusetts 02360
(617) 746-9697

Edwin Smith Historical Museum
6 Elm Street
Westfield, Massachusetts 01085
(413) 568-7833

Wenham Historical Association and
   Museum, Inc.
132 Main Street, Box 64
Wenham, Massachusetts 01984
(617) 468-2377

MICHIGAN

Greenfield Village and Henry Ford
   Museum
Oakwood Boulevard
Dearborn, Michigan 48121
(313) 271-1620

Detroit Institute of Arts
5200 Woodward Avenue
Detroit, Michigan 48202
(313) 833-7900

MISSISSIPPI

Mississippi State Historical Museum
North State and Capitol Streets,
   Box 571
Jackson, Mississippi 39205
(601) 354-6222

MISSOURI

The Saint Louis Art Museum
Forest Park
St. Louis, Missouri 63110
(314) 721-0067

NEW HAMPSHIRE

Manchester Históric Association
129 Amherst Street
Manchester, New Hampshire 03104
(603) 622-7531

New Hampshire Historical Society
30 Park Street
Concord, New Hampshire 03301
(603) 225-3381

NEW JERSEY

Burlington County Historical
   Society
457 High Street
Burlington, New Jersey 08016
(609) 386-4773

Monmouth County Historical
   Association
70 Court Street
Freehold, New Jersey 07728
(201) 462-1466

Morris Museum of Arts and Sciences
Normandy Heights & Columbia
   Roads
Morristown, New Jersey 07960
(201) 538-0454

The Newark Museum
49 Washington Street
Newark, New Jersey 07101
(201) 733-6600

NEW MEXICO

Museum of International Folk Art
706 Camino Lejo, Box 2798
Santa Fe, New Mexico 87503
(505) 827-2544

Museum of New Mexico/Folk Art
   Museum
North Side of the Plaza, Box 2087
Santa Fe, New Mexico 87501
(505) 827-2559

NEW YORK

Albany Institute of History and Art
125 Washington Avenue
Albany, New York 12210
(518) 463-4478

Alling Coverlet Museum
122 William Street
Palmyra, New York 14522
(315) 597-6737

The Brooklyn Museum
188 Eastern Parkway
Brooklyn, New York 11238
(212) 638-5000

"Home Sweet Home" House
14 James Lane
East Hampton, New York 11937
(516) 324-0713

Jefferson County Historical Society
228 Washington Street
Watertown, New York 13601
(315) 782-3491

The Landmark Society Of Western
   New York
130 Spring Street
Rochester, New York 14608
(716) 546-7029

Museum of American Folk Art
49 West 53rd Street
New York, New York 10019
(212) 581-2474

New York State Historical
   Association
Fenimore House, Lake Road
Cooperstown, New York 13326
(607) 547-2533

Schenectady County Historical
   Society
32 Washington Avenue
Schenectady, New York 12305
(518) 374-0263

The Schenectady Museum
Nott Terrace Heights
Schenectady, New York 12308
(518) 382-7890

OHIO

Cincinnati Art Museum
Eden Park
Cincinnati, Ohio 45202
(513) 721-5204

The Massillon Museum
212 Lincoln Way, East
Massillon, Ohio 44646
(216) 833-4061

Ohio Historical Center
Interstate 71 and 17th Avenue
Columbus, Ohio 43211
(614) 466-1500

PENNSYLVANIA

Historical Society of York County
250 East Market Street
York, Pennsylvania 17403
(717) 848-1587

Independence National Historical
Park
313 Walnut Street
Philadelphia, Pennsylvania 19106
(215) 597-7086

Old Economy Village
Fourteenth and Church Streets
Ambridge, Pennsylvania 15003
(412) 266-4500

William Penn Memorial Museum
North and Third Streets
Harrisburg, Pennsylvania 17120
(717) 787-4980

Philadelphia Museum of Art
Twenty-sixth Street and Benjamin
Franklin Parkway
Box 7646
Philadelphia, Pennsylvania 19101
(215) 763-8100

Wyoming Historical and Geological
Society
69 South Franklin Street
Wilkes-Barre, Pennsylvania 18701
(717) 823-6244

RHODE ISLAND

Newport Historical Society
82 Truro Street
Newport, Rhode Island 02840
(401) 846-0813

Rhode Island Historical Society
52 Power Street
Providence, Rhode Island 02906
(401) 331-8575

SOUTH CAROLINA

Charleston Museum
360 Meeting Street
Charleston, South Carolina 29403
(803) 722-2996

TEXAS

Harris County Heritage Society
1100 Bagby
Houston, Texas 77002
(713) 223-8367

Log Cabin Historical Complex
Log Cabin Village Lane and University Drive
Fort Worth, Texas 76109
(817) 926-5881

Witte Memorial Museum
3801 Broadway
San Antonio, Texas 78209
(512) 826-0647

VERMONT

Shelburne Museum
U.S. Route 7
Shelburne, Vermont 05482
(802) 985-3346

VIRGINIA

Valentine Museum
1015 East Clay Street
Richmond, Virginia 23219
(804) 649-0711

WASHINGTON

Eastern Washington State Historical
Society
West 2316 First Avenue
Spokane, Washington 99204
(509) 456-3931

WYOMING

Bradford Brinton Memorial
Museum
Box 23-Quarter Circle A Ranch
Big Horn, Wyoming 82833
(307) 672-3173

Bibliography

Alfers, Betty. *Quilting*. Indianapolis: Bobbs-Merrill Co., Inc., 1978.

Anders, Nedda C. *Appliqué Old and New*. Great Neck, N.Y.: Hearthside Press, 1967.

Bacon, Lenice Ingram. *American Patchwork Quilts*. New York: William Morrow, 1973.

Bannister, Barbara. *The United States Pattern Patchwork Book*. New York: Dover Publications, Inc., 1976.

Beyer, Alice. *Quilting*. Reprint of 1934 edition. Albany, Ca.: East Bay Heritage Quilters, 1978.

Beyer, Jinny. *Patchwork Patterns*. McLean, Va.: EPM Publications, Inc., 1979.

_____. *The Quilter's Album of Blocks and Borders*. McLean, Va.: EPM Publications, Inc., 1980.

Bishop, Robert. *Quilts, Coverlets, Rugs & Samplers*. New York: Alfred A. Knopf, 1982.

Bishop, Robert and Elizabeth Safanda. *A Gallery of Amish Quilts: Design and Diversity from a Plain People*. New York: Dutton Paperbacks, 1975.

Bonesteel, Georgia. *Lap Quilting with Georgia Bonesteel*. Birmingham, Al.: Oxmoor House, Inc., 1982.

Brightbill, Dorothy. *Quilting as a Hobby*. New York: Sterling Publishing Co., 1963.

_____ Carroll, Amy, ed. *Patchwork and Appliqué*. New York: Ballantine Books, 1981.

Colby, Averil. *Patchwork*. Watertown, Mass.: Charles T. Branford Co., 1958.

_____. *Patchwork Quilts*. New York: Charles Scribner's Sons, 1966.

_____. *Quilting*. New York: Charles Scribner's Sons, 1971.

Cooper, Patricia and Norma B. Buferd. *Quilters: Women and Domestic Arts*. New York: Doubleday, 1978.

Dunton, William Rush. *Old Quilts*. Catonsville, Md.: privately published, 1946.

Echols, Margit. *The New American Quilt*. New York: Doubleday & Co., Inc., 1976.

Finley, Ruth E. *Old Patchwork Quilts and the Women Who Made Them*. Watertown, Mass.: Charles T. Branford Co., 1971.

Fisher, Katharine. *Quilting in Squares*. New York: Charles Scribner's Sons, 1978.

Fitzrandolph, Mavis and Florence M. Fletcher. *Quilting*. Woodbridge, N.J.: The Dryad Press, 1972.

Gammell, Alice I. *Polly Prindles' Book of American Patchwork Quilts*. New York: Grosset & Dunlap, Inc., 1973.

Gutcheon, Beth. *The Perfect Patchwork Primer*. New York: David McKay Co., Inc., 1973.

Gutcheon, Beth and Jeffrey. *The Quilt Design Workbook*. New York: Rawson Associates Publishers, Inc., 1976.

Haas, Louise Krause and Robert Bartlett. *Quilts, Counterpanes and Related Fabrics*. Santa Monica, Ca.: Coromandel House, 1956.

Haders, Phyllis. *The Main Street Pocket Guide to Quilts*. Pittstown, N.J.: The Main Street Press, 1983.

_____. *Sunshine and Shadow: The Amish and Their Quilts*. New York: Universe Books, 1976.

Hall, Carrie A. and Rose Kretsinger. *The Romance of the Patchwork Quilt in America*. Reprint of 1935 edition. New York: Bonanza Books, n.d.

Harbeson, Georgiana Brown. *American Needlework*. New York: Bonanza Books, 1938, 1970.

Hinson, Dolores A. *The Quilter's Companion*. New York: Arco Publishing Co., Inc., 1973.

_____. *Quilter's Manual*. New York: Hearthside Press, 1970.

Holstein, Jonathan. *Abstract Design in American Quilts*. New York: Whitney Museum of American Art, 1971.

_____. *The Pieced Quilt*. Greenwich, Conn.: New York Graphic Society, 1973.

Houck, Carter and Myron Miller. *American Quilts and How to Make Them*. New York: Charles Scribner's Sons, 1975.

Ickis, Marguerite. *The Standard Book of Quilt Making and Collecting.* New York: Dover Publications Inc., 1949.

Ives, Suzy. *Patterns for Patchwork Quilts and Cushions.* Watertown, Mass.: Charles T. Branford, 1977.

Johnson, Mary Elizabeth. *Prize Country Quilts.* Birmingham, Al.: Oxmoor House, Inc., 1977.

Jones, Stella. *Hawaiian Quilts.* Honolulu: Honolulu Academy of Arts, 1930.

Khin, Yvonne. *The Collector's Dictionary of Quilt Names & Patterns.* Washington, D.C.: Acropolis Books, Ltd., 1980.

Lewis, Alfred Allen. *The Mountain Artisan's Quilting Book.* New York: Macmillan & Co., 1973.

Lithgow, Marilyn. *Quiltmaking and Quiltmakers.* New York: Thomas Y. Crowell Co., 1974.

Mainardi, Patricia. *Quilts: The Great American Art.* San Pedro, Ca.: Miles and Weir, 1978.

Marston, Doris E. *Patchwork Today.* Watertown, Mass.: Charles T. Branford Co., 1968.

McCosh, Elizabeth. *Introduction to Patchwork.* New York: Taplinger, 1962.

McKain, Sharon. *The Great Noank Quilt Factory.* New York: Random House, 1974.

McKim, Ruby. *One Hundred and One Patchwork Patterns.* New York: Dover Publications, Inc., 1962.

Newman, Thelma R. *Quilting, Patchwork, Appliqué and Trapunto: Traditional Methods and Original Designs.* New York: Crown Publishers, Inc., 1974.

Orlofsky, Patsy and Myron. *Quilts in America.* New York: McGraw-Hill Book Co., 1974.

Paddleford, Clementine. *Patchwork Quilts: A Collection of Forty-One Old Time Blocks.* New York: Farm and Fireside, n.d.

Peto, Florence. *American Quilts and Coverlets.* New York: Chanticleer Press, 1949.

_____. *Historic Quilts.* New York: American Historical Co., Inc., 1939.

Robertson, Elizabeth Wells. *American Quilts.* New York: The Studio Publications, 1948.

Roesler, John. *Rectangular Quilt Blocks.* Des Moines: Wallace-Homestead Book Co., 1983.

Safford, Carleton L. and Robert Bishop. *America's Quilts and Coverlets.* New York: E.P. Dutton, Inc., 1972.

Sommer, Elyse with Joellen Sommer. *A Patchwork, Appliqué and Quilting Primer.* New York: Lothrop, Lee & Shepard Co., 1975.

Stevens, Napua. *The Hawaiian Quilt.* Honolulu: Service Printers, 1971.

Timmins, Alice. *Patchwork Simplified.* New York: Arco Publishing Co., Inc., 1975.

Vogue Guide to Patchwork and Quilting. New York: Condé Nast, 1973.

Webster, Marie D. *Quilts—Their Story and How to Make Them.* Reprint of 1915 edition. New York: Tudor Publishing Co., 1948.

Wilson, Erica. *Erica Wilson's Quilts of America.* Birmingham, Al.: Oxmoor House, Inc., 1979.

Woodard, Thomas K. and Blanche Greenstein. *Crib Quilts and Other Small Wonders.* New York: E.P. Dutton, Inc., 1981.

Index

The quilts illustrated in this book are in the possession of Tewksbury Antiques, Oldwick, N.J., with the following exceptions: Crossbars, Wild Goose Chase, and Grandmother's Flower Garden (The Pink House); Tumbling Blocks, House, and Peapod Leaf (Phyllis Haders); Windmill Blades, Sunshine and Shadow, and Barn Raising (Morris Museum of Arts and Sciences); Tree of Life and Star of Bethlehem (Mr. and Mrs. William D. Blaine); Drunkard's Path and Nine-Patch (Karen Wiss); Wedding Ring (Linda McKenna and Nacky Smith Morgan); Sailboat (Mr. and Mrs. Alan E. Burland); Sugar Loaf (Jack and Sonja Perry), and Amish Bars (1800 House).

The black and white illustrations of various Amish Bar designs on pp. 124-25 are reproduced, in order of appearance, through the courtesy of Esprit de Corps, Phyllis Haders, Darwin Bearley, and Phyllis Haders.